GW00392943

JOAN SUTHERLAND

◇ A TRIBUTE ◇

MOFFATT OXENBOULD

Introductions by
Richard Bonynge &
The Earl of Harewood

 Art Gallery of New South Wales

 HONEYSETT PUBLICATIONS

© Copyright 1989 Honeysett Publications Pty Limited
   & Art Gallery of New South Wales
© Copyright 1989 Text, Moffatt Oxenbould

Published by Honeysett Publications Pty Limited
PO Box 23, Westgate NSW 2048 Australia

Produced by The Honeysett Printing Group
Tel (02) 569 8133   Fax (02) 560 5925

Edited by Alan Davies, George Jaksic, Warren Wickman & Andrew Wilson

Artwork and Digital Typesetting – Honeysett Typesetters Pty Limited
Concept design – Spatchurst Design Associates
Cover design – Alan Hancock
Photography – Cover, costumes and copying – Greg Weight, Sydney
Photolithography – Prestige Plates Pty Limited
Printing – Griffin Press Limited
Typography design – Typeface Research Pty Limited

National Library of Australia
Cataloguing-in-Publication data:

   Oxenbould, Moffatt Benjamin 1943-

   JOAN SUTHERLAND: A TRIBUTE

      Bibliography

      ISBN 0 9592229 6 0

      1. Sutherland, Dame Joan, 1926-
      2. Opera – Biography
      3. Opera – Pictorial Works
      I. Honeysett Publications Pty Limited
      II. Title

This book is copyright. Apart from any fair dealing for the purposes of private
study, research, criticism or review as permitted under the Copyright Act, no
part may be reproduced, stored in a retrieval system or transmitted in any form
or by any means, electronic, mechanical, photocopying, recording or otherwise
without prior written permission. Enquiries should be made to the publishers.

First Published 1989

TABLE OF CONTENTS

FOREWORD

RADIANT IS a word which amply describes Dame Joan Sutherland, not only on the stage but also off-stage. The exhibition and the accompanying book are designed to pay tribute to her extraordinary and inspiring contribution to opera and to her as a truly outstanding human being of whom Australia is justly proud and to whom we are all devoted.

This whole project, which I suppose falls slightly outside the normal range of activities for an art museum, is one which we initiated simply because of our admiration for Joan Sutherland. It would not have been possible without the fullest support and co-operation of both Dame Joan and Richard Bonynge to whom I express our great thanks, not only for bearing with us, but also for lending so much of the documentary and ancilliary material which has been furnished from the Bonynge's own collection.

To The Australian Opera, Moffatt Oxenbould, Diana Heath, the other lenders and all the sponsors and supporters, our thanks for assisting the Gallery in realising this unique event.

Edmund Capon
Director,
Art Gallery of NSW
Sydney, December 1989.

Portrait Sketch of Joan Sutherland by Louis Kahan, Melbourne 1965.

PREFACE

DAME JOAN SUTHERLAND is at the Opera Centre in Surry Hills, Sydney, headquarters of The Australian Opera. It is August 1989. She has come to join in the farewell festivities for an Australian Opera singer, her long time friend and colleague, Elizabeth Allen, who is leaving the chorus of the Company.

It is more than thirty years since Joan Surtherland first came to international prominence with her debut as Lucia di Lammermoor at the Royal Opera House, Covent Garden. It is now approaching the time when this great singer will give her final performances in Sydney in 1990, London and Barcelona in 1991.

Dame Joan has come early to the Opera Centre to 'clear out' her wardrobe skip – the large cane basket in which has been stored the paraphernalia of her Australian dressing rooms – makeup, dressing gowns, hairbrushes, some stage jewellery and the like. As we leave the Artists' Green Room, where the farewell party has been an affectionate and sincere celebration for a stalwart chorister, Dame Joan tells me of her afternoon's work and says that The Australian Opera now has a spare wardrobe basket to put to other use. It is a strangely upsetting moment, the first real acceptance for me that the farewell, which has been talked about for some time is actually a reality and that after **Les Huguenots** in October 1990, there will be no more Australian theatre performances given by one of the greatest sopranos of all time.

I remember as an opera-crazed schoolboy reading of her Lucia triumph in London in 1959. I remember the excitement of first hearing her voice on record soon after and the much greater excitement of hearing her rehearse Lucia for her triumphant return to Australia in 1965, the final night of **La Sonnambula** in Melbourne, the same year she sang 'Home Sweet Home' at the audience's insistence during the curtain calls. I recall many subsequent performances, in London, San Francisco, New York and particularly in Australia.

These memories are the more vivid because I have been working as curator for the Art Gallery of New South Wales' **Joan Sutherland: A Tribute** exhibition and have been retrospectively looking at her career in connection with this exhibition for some months. I realise, suddenly, that I have taken for granted this voice and this artist. I have been privileged to hear her often, to work with her over a long period of time and to have her as a friend. I know that at the flick of a switch, present and future generations will be able to hear and see Joan Sutherland perform 'electronically', but I realise just how privileged I have been and how privileged Australians have been to have heard this great artist in so

Moffatt Oxenbould
Artistic Director,
The Australian Opera
Sydney, December 1989.

◐ *Curtain Call after a performance of* Anna Bolena, *Royal Opera House Covent Garden London 1988.*

much of her repertoire over the period in which she has also been acclaimed in the great operatic centres of the world.

The voice of Joan Sutherland is God-given and what has been done with this gift is recalled in the following pages, which trace her career from the secretary singing at music clubs and winning competitions in post-Second World War Sydney to the stages of Covent Garden, La Scala and the Metropolitan Opera in New York.

Joan Sutherland has been fortunate to have as a life partner Richard Bonynge, who heard the potential of her voice and encouraged her to sing the great *bel canto* roles of the nineteenth century, carrying on the tradition of the great divas of the past: Malibran, Pasta, Lind, Patti and Melba. Richard Bonynge has guided his wife's career across an extraordinarily wide repertoire which she has approached with the integrity and discipline which characterise her as an artist.

Not only as a great interpreter does she serve as a model to present and future generations. Joan Sutherland has, throughout her career, believed in giving her audience the very best of which she is capable. To ensure her own high standards, she has set herself strict disciplines regarding rehearsal and performance and these disciplines have ensured that hers has been a long association with some of the most demanding roles created for the soprano voice.

► *Costume design by Michael Stennett for Joan Sutherland as Amalia in* I Masnadieri *for The Australian Opera production in 1980.*

INTRODUCTION

A CAREER that has spanned 42 years is surely something of a phenomenon in the operatic world. Joan herself tends to belittle her achievements – she was given a voice by God, she worked hard, learned to sing properly and kept on singing.

But how many voices throughout history have been able to encompass a wide and amazingly diverse repertoire – sing constantly for forty years in the great opera houses of the world and survive?

In her sixties she is still singing Norma, Lucrezia Borgia and Lucia in huge theatres. Her long career has encompassed the baroque operas of Handel, Haydn and Mozart – the nineteenth century Italian and French operas ranging from the romantic to the *verismo* – Rossini, Bellini, Donizetti, Verdi, Puccini and Cilea in the Italian school, Weber and Wagner in the German school, Gounod, Delibes and Massenet in the French, with a few forays into operetta and a big recital repertoire. She sang much modern music, both in the theatre and concert hall, by Britten, Tippett, Walton, Honneger, Frank Martin and Poulenc. Not to forget in excess of forty complete opera recordings and countless discs of arias and songs. Many of the operas which she sang had not been heard in this century or certainly not for fifty years.

Why did this voice survive when so many careers today are so short and survive singing such diverse roles – Aida and Olympia, Turandot and Lucia, Eva and Norma?

I can only imagine that it is because her technique of singing was begun and nurtured in the school of *bel canto*. And what, we are constantly asked, is *bel canto*? So many books have been written about it, but it almost belies description. It unites the three natural registers of the voice – the chest, middle and head – into one. It demands a seamless *legato*, a *coloratura* technique and absolute control of dynamics. It requires a beautiful sound. The size of the voice has nothing to do with it – all categories of voice are improved with training and Joan was fortunate in that her mother had studied with Burns Walker, a pupil of Marchesi, herself a pupil of Manuel Garcia who was Rossini's first Almaviva in **The Barber of Seville**. From an early age she was exposed to the right method.

But method is not enough. One must be born with an instinct for singing and this can rarely be taught – only developed. Although there are hundreds of books on the subject, I defy anyone to conquer this art by reading them. Joan conquered this art because of an inner strength, a tenacity of purpose, an enormous self-discipline and a great heart.

She learned, she sang and she endures. She is a strong lady who realised her potential and in the entire world she is probably the one least conscious of it.

Richard Bonynge
Sydney, December 1989.

🜄 *Joan Sutherland and Richard Bonynge after a recording session 1988.*

◉ *Costume design by Michael Stennett for Joan Sutherland as Ophélie in* Hamlet, *Canadian Opera 1985.*

A PERSONAL VIEW

I BELIEVE the grandest exponents in the second half of the twentieth century of what we usually call *bel canto* – that outlook on singing which is somehow quintessentially Italian, but by no means exclusively practised by Italians – have been the Greek Maria Callas and the Australian Joan Sutherland. Joan was born two years and 11 months after Maria and yet her career still flourishes 12 years after her colleague died and 23 years after Callas last sang opera.

Sutherland and Callas sang together only twice, both times in London, in **Norma** in 1952 and later in a Gala in 1958. The first time, the one was a celebrity making her British debut and the other was in one of her first stage roles; the next, Callas was the world's reigning prima donna, Sutherland about to become the leading contender for her throne. Joan, who was always pragmatic and confident, would not have seen it like that, but Maria possibly did, not in an unpleasant way (as the world and its press might have preferred) but because Joan in rehearsal caught her unerring ear and made her sit up and take notice as she otherwise did, in my experience, only when listening to records of Rosa Ponselle – or to her own.

As often with performing artists, comparisons are imprecise and useful only to point up tremendous achievement. Sutherland and Callas are not alike as singers, but they often sang the same music and they made their careers in the same musical areas. All the same, if Maria Callas is a modern singer in a traditional repertory, Joan Sutherland is a modern example of an older school. Maria's characteristic was the ability to explore an opera's text, musical and verbal, to extract meaning the listener had not dared to believe was there. Joan's virtues, which she has for more than thirty years possessed as perhaps no-one else, lie in the regions of sovereign technical control, leading to certainty of vocal execution, to pure, limpid, treasurable tone, to beautifully secure, powerful top notes. Callas did not possess that security. Does that make Sutherland sound dull? I don't think so; nor was she.

The Sutherland technique has not led to blandness, rather to a grandeur of phrasing, an illuminating radiance of sound, qualities not only rare in themselves, but revealing beauties in scores which no-one any longer knew they possessed. Callas started to explore the Italian repertory of the nineteenth Century, but it was left to Sutherland (and later to Montserrat Caballé) to make discoveries only hinted at in the decade of Callas' ascendancy. And in a way, we have all taken this for granted, because with Joan, as with all great athletes – singers are, among other things, athletes – it seems less difficult than it is.

I am a lover of gramophone records and Sutherland is one of the great prodigies of the black disc era. I have several times for a record review compared all the records of a particular opera (and I mean all) and

The Earl of Harewood
London, December 1989.

⬧ *Costume design by Michael Stennett for Joan Sutherland as* Anna Bolena, Act One Scene One.

This article originally appeared in The Age *in Melbourne on 8 November 1986 at the time of Joan Sutherland's 60th Birthday.*

⬤ *Costume design by Michael Stennett for Joan Sutherland as* Anna Bolena, *Act One Scene Three.*

this has sometimes meant listening to between 50 and 100 different versions of an aria recorded over a period of 75 or 80 years. If it is a tenor aria and Caruso has recorded it, almost never have I found more than perhaps a couple of versions in which I could conceivably find virtues preferable to his and the same for soprano pieces consistently applies to Sutherland – oddly enough, I have never written about any of the dozens of complete operas she has recorded. The idea of perfection (it can be no more) constantly suggests itself when one hears her recorded performances; it's not just polish or an absence of blemish, but something much more positive, much more authoritative – and much more enjoyable.

Listening to records, you find perhaps a point of genuine comparison with Callas. Both voices are genuinely big, dominating instruments and the scale of the singing is an important part of the quality of each of these great sopranos.

For no fewer than 36 years, Joan Sutherland has given me personally more consistent pleasure than any other great singer. It was in 1954 when I first heard her sing Antonia in a new Covent Garden production of **The Tales of Hoffmann** that I knew she had the possibility of greatness and the glory of her phrasing and the exuberance of those top notes used every night to send the audience into transports of delight. Her musical prowess I first recognised when she sang an admirable Lady Rich in Britten's Coronation Opera **Gloriana** a few weeks after its 1953 premiere and when she sang Jenifer in the first performance of Tippett's **The Midsummer Marriage** in 1955.

I don't know whether those nights are among Joan's happier memories, but they are among mine; technique, attack and tone adorned those modern scores, just as surely as they were soon after to adorn the music composed for Micaela, Desdemona, Alcina and then, most notably of all, Lucia, at whose first performance in 1959 a star was more evidently born than on any other night in my operatic experience. The conductor Tullio Serafin that night gave her musical confidence, Franco Zeffirelli new stage dynamism and Richard Bonynge had left her in no doubt about her ability to sing the role as no one alive. For the ensuing 30 years, whether she sang Queen Marguerite in **Les Huguenots** at La Scala, or Amina in **La Sonnambula** at Covent Garden, or Esclarmonde in San Francisco, or a dozen roles in Australia, Joan has remained without peer: an exhilarating singer.

My own professional work has on the whole been in a neighbouring but not precisely similar field of operatic endeavour, that of ensemble opera. But I think there is no fundamental paradox in a love of fine singing and a conviction that opera is ultimately to do with music-theatre. At great moments, now as in time past, they coincide. I was at **I Puritani** one night at the Metropolitan in New York and when Joan had sung *'Son vergin vezzosa'*, my neighbour, a professional singer and a close friend, whispered to me, 'There is nobody else who can sing it like that!' I said. 'I am dedicated to exactly the opposite proposition!' – but in my heart I knew he was right. Moreover, with the exception of Maria Callas, probably nobody but Joan could have made me admit that!

AUSTRALIA

JOAN SUTHERLAND was born in Sydney on 7 November 1926. She was educated at St Catherine's Church of England School for Girls, in the Sydney suburb of Waverley, which she left at the age of 16. Her mother Muriel Sutherland had a mezzo-soprano voice of quality and instilled in Joan the joy of singing. Her first appearances were with the Affiliated Music Clubs of New South Wales and she was occasionally accompanied at concerts by Richard Bonynge, a gifted piano student at the New South Wales State Conservatorium of Music. In 1949 she gave up her job as a secretary to concentrate on singing; she won the Sydney *Sun* Aria competition in 1949 and the Mobil Quest in 1950. In April 1951 a farewell benefit concert at the Sydney Town Hall was organised by the Vacuum Oil Company and Associated Newspapers, and prior to her departure for further study and a hoped for career in London, Joan made her first staged operatic appearance at the New South Wales State Conservatorium of Music in the title role of Eugene Goossens' opera **Judith**. In July 1951, accompanied by her mother, Joan Sutherland sailed from Sydney on the *Maloja*.

⬤ Advertising leaflet for the New South Wales State Conservatorium of Music 1951 Opera Season of — Judith *(Goossens) and* Gianni Schicchi *(Puccini). Joan Sutherland sang the title role in* Judith.

⬤ Joan Sutherland singing at the Mobil Quest Finalists' Concert at the Assembly Hall in Sydney, 20 September 1950. Photograph by Milton Kent.

⬤ Advertising leaflet for the Joan Sutherland Farewell Concert held in Sydney on 20 April 1951.

⬤ Joan Sutherland c. 1927.

N.S.W. STATE CONSERVATORIUM OF MUSIC

Director: EUGENE GOOSSENS, D.Mus., F.R.C.M.

OPERA SEASON

1951

SATURDAY, 9TH JUNE.
SATURDAY, 16TH JUNE.
FRIDAY, 22ND JUNE.

TUESDAY, 12TH JUNE
MONDAY, 18TH JUNE
TUESDAY, 26TH JUNE

(All Performances commence at 8 p.m.)

Complete Stage Presentation of

The Dramatic Opera

JUDITH

(GOOSSENS)

and The Comic Opera

GIANNI SCHICCHI

(PUCCINI)

(Both for the first time in Australia.)

CONDUCTORS: EUGENE GOOSSENS, NOEL NICKSON.
PRODUCTION: HILDA MULLIGAN, NINO MAROTTA AND
THE DIRECTOR.
SCENIC ARTIST: WILLIAM CONSTABLE.
BALLET ARRANGED BY RAISSA KOUSNETZOVA.
GENERAL ORGANISER: ROLAND FOSTER, F.G.S.M.

FULL ORCHESTRA.

SPECIALLY DESIGNED COSTUMES AND SCENIC SETTINGS.

Casts Include:

"JUDITH":

JOAN SUTHERLAND, HEATHER McMILLAN, JAMES WILSON,
LINA BELLE, MARY ADAMS, RONALD DOWD, ALAN LIGHT.

"GIANNI SCHICCHI":

FRANK LISLE, ARETE ZANTIOTIS, MARY ADAMS, ALAN FERRIS,
ROLANDO LUCANTONIO, PATRICIA MOORE, DAVID BARWELL,
JOHN YOUNG, ALAN LIGHT, RENEE GOOSSENS, GEOFFREY
CHARD, WILLIAM DIAMOND.

RESERVED 7/6 AND 5/—   UNRESERVED 2/6

Plans for first performance at NICHOLSON'S and PALING'S from
THURSDAY, 31ST MAY. Other plans available ten
days before the performance.

R. G. ALLINGHAM, Registrar.

JOAN SUTHERLAND (Dramatic Soprano)
Winner 1949 "Sun Aria" Competition
Winner 1950 "Mobil Quest"

JOAN SUTHERLAND

FAREWELL CONCERT

SYDNEY TOWN HALL

FRIDAY, 20th APRIL, 1951

8 p.m.

———

Supporting Artists include:—

MARIE VAN HOVE	(Pianiste)
FLORENCE TAYLOR	(Contralto)
RONALD DOWD	(Tenor)
FRANK W. LISLE	(Bass)
BRENTON LANGBEIN	(Violinist)
AIDA SUMMERS / ADRIAN HOLLAND	(Accompanists)

(All supporting artists have donated their services)

———

TICKETS: Reserved, 7/6, 5/3; Unreserved, 3/—
(All prices include tax)

———

PLAN: Palings and Nicholsons

A PROGRAMME OF POPULAR APPEAL — PROCEEDS IN AID OF MISS SUTHERLAND'S OVERSEAS STUDIES

LONDON

WHEN A hopeful Joan Sutherland arrived in London in August 1951, Professor Clive Carey of the Royal College of Music was impressed with her potential and recommended that she study for a year at the College Opera School. Richard Bonynge was also a student at the College, and in addition to his piano studies, had continued to study the operatic repertoire, particularly the *bel canto* operas of the nineteenth century. He believed that Joan Sutherland had the ability to sing these operas and that she possessed a much greater vocal range and flexibility than had hitherto been imagined.

In 1952 Joan sang Giorgetta in Puccini's **Il Tabarro** in a Royal College of Music student performance; and in October, after three separate auditions, she became a member of the Company of the Royal Opera House Covent Garden, whose General Administrator was David Webster.

Joan Sutherland's debut at the Royal Opera House was on 28 October 1952 as the First Lady in **Die Zauberflöte**. On 3 November she sang the Priestess in **Aida**, conducted by Sir John Barbirolli and on 8 November sang Clotilde in a new production of Bellini's **Norma**, in which the title role was sung by Maria Callas, for whom many of the great *bel canto* operas were being revived in major theatres. The legendary mezzo-soprano Ebe Stignani sang Adalgisa in these performances.

In December 1952 Joan Sutherland sang her first leading role with the Royal Opera, that of Amelia in Verdi's **Un Ballo in Maschera** in which she substituted at short notice for an ailing scheduled artist. Other roles at Covent Garden followed, and David Webster arranged for Joan to work with Norman Ayrton, an experienced director and teacher, on stage technique and movement. In 1953 Joan went with the Royal Opera to Rhodesia for the Rhodes Centenary Celebrations, singing the role of Lady Penelope Rich in Britten's **Gloriana**, the Priestess and covering the title role in **Aida** and the Countess in **Le Nozze di Figaro**.

On 16 October 1954 Joan Sutherland and Richard Bonynge were married at Kensington Methodist Church.

⬥ *Joan Sutherland as Agathe in* Der Freischütz, *Royal Opera House Covent Garden, 1954. Photograph by Dennis de Marney.*

◗ *Costume designed by Alan Barlow and worn by Joan Sutherland as Clotilde in* Norma, *at the Royal Opera House Covent Garden, in 1952. Photograph by Greg Weight.*

⬥ *Joan Sutherland as Clotilde in* Norma, *London 1952, with Maria Callas as Norma, the celebrated Italian mezzo-soprano Ebe Stignani as Adalgisa and Michael Kelly and Michael Nicholls as the two children of Norma and Pollione. Photograph by Roger Wood.*

OPERA COMPANY LEAVE FOR AFRICA. Some of the members of the Covent Garden Opera Company at Airways Terminal, Victoria, yesterday, when they left for Southern Rhodesia to present opera at the newly constructed Theatre Royal, Bulawayo, as part of the Rhodes Centenary celebrations. They are (LEFT TO RIGHT): Mr. Eric Mitchell, Miss Elizabeth Latham (stage manager), Mr. Frederick Dalberg, Miss Joan Sutherland, Mr. Norman Walker, Miss Constance Shacklock and Mr. Jesse Walters.

◐ *Joan Sutherland as Frasquita in* Carmen *with Nell Rankin as Carmen, Barbara Howitt as Mercedes, David Tree as Remendado and Edmund Donleavy as Dancairo. Photograph by Roger Wood.*

◑ *Costume worn by Joan Sutherland as Giulietta, designed by Jose Varona for The Australian Opera in 1974. Photograph by Greg Weight.*

◓ *Joan Sutherland departing for Rhodesia with members of the Covent Garden Company at the airways terminal, Victoria Station. From left to right: Eric Mitchell, Elizabeth Latham, Frederick Dalberg, Joan Sutherland, Norman Walker, Constance Shacklock and Jess Walters.*

◒ *Costume design by John Piper for Lady Penelope Rich in* Gloriana, *the opera by Benjamin Britten, which was first performed in London in 1953, at the time of the coronation.*

◑ *Joan Sutherland as Lady Penelope Rich in* Gloriana, *in 1953.*

TALES OF HOFFMANN

LONDON SAW Joan Sutherland's debut in Offenbach's **Les Contes d'Hoffmann**. In November 1954 she sang the role of Antonia at the Royal Opera House Covent Garden in a production conducted by Edward Downes, directed by Gunther Rennert and designed by Georges Wakhevitch. Sutherland shared the role with another Australian soprano, Elsie Morison. On 28 February 1955 she sang Giulietta on tour with the Royal Opera in Glasgow and on 16 June the same year sang Olympia at the Royal Opera House in London. There were further performances of Antonia in London in 1956 and 1957.

In 1970 Joan Sutherland sang all four soprano roles – Olympia, Giulietta, Antonia and Stella – in a new production in Seattle of Richard Bonynge's performing version of Offenbach's work. Richard Bonynge conducted with Bliss Hebert as director and Alan Charles Klein as designer. Joan's costumes were designed by Jose Varona. She sang all four roles at the Metropolitan Opera in New York in 1973 and 1974 in what was essentially the Seattle production, and with the Metropolitan Opera on tour in 1974 in Detroit, Atlanta, Memphis, Dallas and Minneapolis.

In 1974 Joan Sutherland and Richard Bonynge returned to Australia for the first time since 1965 to perform with The Australian Opera. The opera chosen was **Les Contes d'Hoffmann**, conducted by Richard Bonynge, directed by Tito Capobianco and designed by Jose Varona. In 1984 the production was revived by Tito Capobianco with Joan again singing all four soprano roles to mark the tenth anniversary of her first Australian Opera appearances.

In January 1985 Sutherland sang all four roles in the Esso Opera in the Park performance in the Sydney Domain.

▶ *Costume design for Joan Sutherland as Giulietta by Jose Varona for The Australian Opera in 1974.*

▲ *Curtain Call after the first performance of the Tito Capobianco production of Les Contes d'Hoffmann in Sydney in 1974 with Raymond Myers as Lindorf, Richard Bonynge, Joan Sutherland, John Winther and Henri Wilden as Hoffmann.*

▲ *Joan Sutherland as Olympia in Sydney 1984, with Horst Hoffmann as Hoffmann, in The Australian Opera's revival of Les Contes d'Hoffmann, to celebrate the tenth anniversary of the company's association with Joan Sutherland and Richard Bonynge. Photograph by Branco Gaica.*

▲ *Costume design by Georges Wakhevitch for Elsie Morison and Joan Sutherland as Antonia in Les Contes d'Hoffmann, Royal Opera House Covent Garden, 1954.*

◀ *Joan Sutherland as Olympia in Les Contes d'Hoffman at the Royal Opera House Covent Garden, London 1955.*

#35 Giulietta

J. Varona
NY. 73

PRINCIPAL SOPRANO

THE LEADING soprano role of Jenifer in Michael Tippett's opera *The Midsummer Marriage* was sung by Joan Sutherland in London on 27 January 1955, and in the same year she sang performances of Antonia, Olympia, Agathe in *Der Freischütz* and the Priestess in *Aida*. In 1954 she had sung a single performance of the title role in *Aida*, and in 1955 repeated the role in Glasgow, Manchester and London for a few performances. On 20 October she sang her first performance of Micaela in *Carmen* at the Royal Opera House Covent Garden.

On 13 February 1956 Adam Bonynge was born in London at Queen Charlotte's Hospital. Joan Sutherland's Glyndebourne Festival debut was on 6 July 1956 as Countess Almaviva in *Le Nozze di Figaro*, conducted by Vittorio Gui in a production by Carl Ebert designed by Oliver Messel. At Glyndebourne in the same season she sang the First Lady in *Die Zauberflöte*, later in the year singing Pamina in the same opera at Covent Garden.

In 1957 Joan sang Ėva in a new production of *Die Meistersinger von Nürnberg* at the Royal Opera House, Covent Garden. The opera was conducted by Rafael Kubelik, directed by Erich Witte and designed by Georges Wakhevitch.

♠ *Backstage during a performance of* The Midsummer Marriage *at the Royal Opera House Covent Garden in 1955. Photograph by the Keystone Press Agency.*

♣ *Joan Sutherland as Countess Almaviva in* Le Nozze di Figaro, *Glyndebourne Festival Opera, 1956. Photograph by Guy Gravett.*

♥ *Joan Sutherland as Eva in* Die Meistersinger von Nürnberg, *at the Royal Opera House Covent Garden, in 1957. Photograph by Houston Rogers.*

► *Joan Sutherland as Jenifer in* The Midsummer Marriage, *Royal Opera House Covent Garden, 1955. Photograph by Houston Rogers.*

♦ *Costume design by Georges Wakhevitch for Eva in Act One of* Die Meistersinger von Nürnberg, *for Covent Garden's production of the opera in 1957.*

ALCINA

JOAN SUTHERLAND'S first performance in the title role of **Alcina** was on 19 March 1957 at the St Pancras Town Hall in London, in a presentation by the Handel Opera Society, conducted by Charles Farncombe and directed by Anthony Besch. She sang a broadcast performance of the opera from Cologne in 1959.

Her next performances were those in Venice, which earned her the accolade *La Stupenda*, which has remained with her throughout her subsequent career. The first Venice performance was on 19 February 1960, conducted by Nicola Rescigno, directed by Franco Zeffirelli and designed by Franco Zeffirelli and Anna Anni. This production travelled later in the year to Dallas and in 1962 to London.

In 1965 Joan Sutherland sang Alcina in concert performances in New York at Carnegie Hall. A further concert performance was given in London at the Royal Festival Hall in 1969. Both performances were conducted by Richard Bonynge.

In 1983 Joan Sutherland sang Alcina in staged performances in Sydney with The Australian Opera, conducted by Richard Bonynge, directed by Sir Robert Helpmann and designed by John Pascoe. Joan's costumes for this production were designed and made by Barbara Matera.

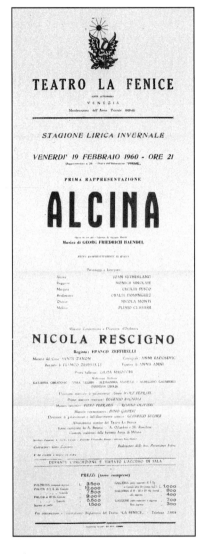

♠ *Poster for* Alcina, *from the Teatro La Fenice, Venice 1960.*

◐ *Joan Sutherland as Alcina in Venice in 1960 with Richard Bonynge, in costume at the harpsichord. Photograph by Foto Film Venezia.*

◑ *Joan Sutherland as Alcina, Handel Opera Society, London 1957. Photograph by A. Dawson.*

◓ *Costume design by Anna Anni for Joan Sutherland as Alcina, in Venice 1960.*

SUTHERLAND

SUTHERLAND

Costume worn by Joan Sutherland as Alcina, Sydney 1983, designed and made by Barbara Matera, for Sir Robert Helpmann's production of Handel's opera. Photograph by Greg Weight.

Joan Sutherland as Alcina with Margreta Elkins as Ruggiero, in The Australian Opera production of Alcina in Sydney, 1983. Photograph by Branco Gaica.

Joan Sutherland as Alcina, Royal Opera House Covent Garden 1962. Photograph by Anthony Crickmay.

BEL CANTO BEGINNINGS

FOLLOWING UPON Olympia, the role of Alcina in 1957 gave indications of the success that Joan Sutherland could achieve in the *bel canto* repertoire. In 1957 she sang her first Gilda in Verdi's **Rigoletto** at Covent Garden, and her first Desdemona in the same composer's **Otello**. At the 1957 Glyndebourne Festival Sutherland sang the role of Madame Herz in Mozart's **Der Schauspieldirektor**, conducted by Bryan Balkwill, directed by Anthony Besch and designed by Peter Rice.

In 1958 Joan Sutherland sang at the Centenary Gala of the Royal Opera House the aria and following duet 'I dreamt I dwelt in marble halls' from Balfe's **The Bohemian Girl**, with John Lanigan. Later in the year she enjoyed a considerable success singing the role of the Israelite Woman in Handel's **Samson** with the Royal Opera, initially at Leeds and then at Covent Garden.

❧ *Souvenir poster programme for the Royal Opera House Centenary Gala, 10 June 1958, in which Joan Sutherland sang excerpts from Michael Balfe's* The Bohemian Girl, *with fellow Australian, John Lanigan.*

❧ *Joan Sutherland as Madame Herz in* Der Schauspieldirektor *at Glyndebourne in 1957, with Naida Labay as Madame Silberklang and Alexander Young as Vogelsang. Photograph by Guy Gravett.*

❧ *Joan Sutherland as Gilda with Otokar Kraus as Rigoletto, at the Royal Opera House, Covent Garden, 1957. Photograph by Barratt's Photo Press.*

❧ *Joan Sutherland as the Israelite Woman in Handel's* Samson, *with John Lanigan as Samson, Royal Opera House Covent Garden, 1958. Photograph by Houston Rogers.*

❧ *Backstage after* Rigoletto *at Covent Garden in 1958, the three Australian principals: Albert Lance (Lance Ingram) as the Duke of Mantua, Joan Sutherland as Gilda and John Shaw as Rigoletto. Photograph by the Keystone Press Agency.*

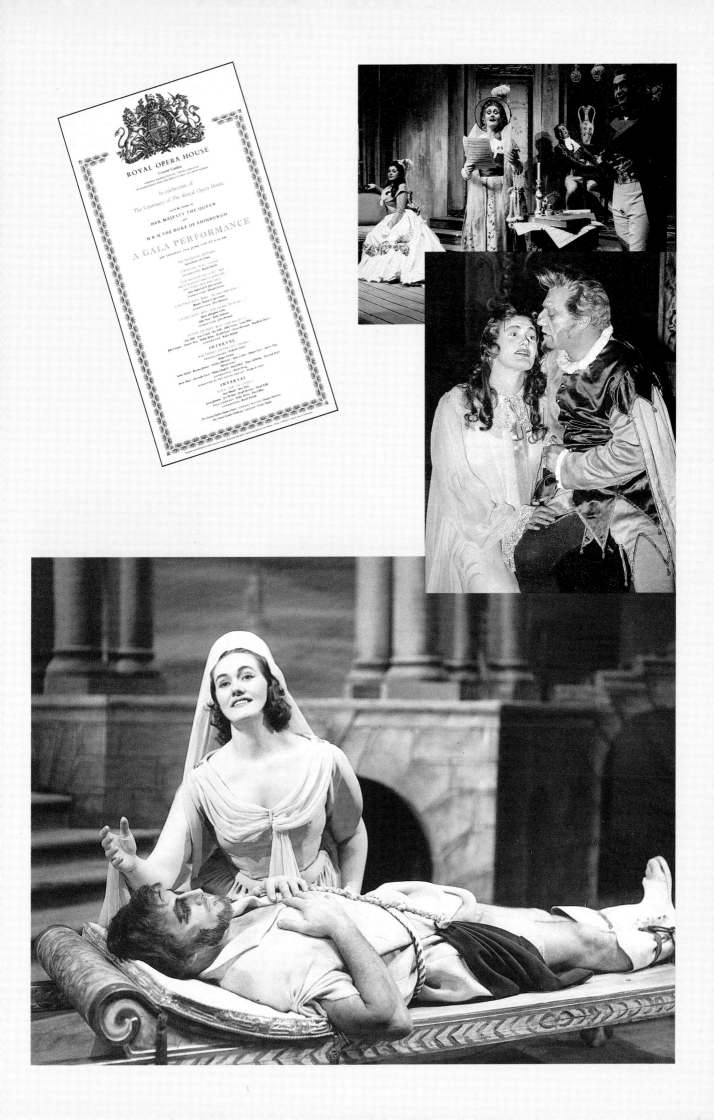

DESDEMONA

VERDI'S OPERA *Otello*, at the Royal Opera House Covent Garden, featured Joan Sutherland singing Desdemona for the first time in December 1957. After her sensational success as **Lucia di Lammermoor** in London in 1959 she was invited that same year to sing two roles at the Staatsoper in Vienna, one of these roles being Desdemona.

In 1981 she returned to the role of Desdemona in Sydney and Melbourne in a new Australian Opera production of **Otello**, conducted by Carlo Felice Cillario, directed by George Ogilvie and designed by Kristian Fredrikson and Shaun Gurton.

⬥ *Joan Sutherland as Desdemona in Act Three of* Otello *with Angelo Marenzi as Otello, in The Australian Opera's 1981 production. Photograph by Branco Gaica.*

◗ *Costume designed by Kristian Fredrikson and worn by Joan Sutherland as Desdemona in Act Three of The Australian Opera's production of* Otello *in 1981. Photograph by Greg Weight.*

◗ *Joan Sutherland as Desdemona in Verdi's* Otello, *Vienna 1959. Photograph by Fayer & Co.*

MADAME LIDOINE

BRITAIN'S FIRST performance of Poulenc's opera **Dialogues des Carmelites** was presented on 16 January 1958 at the Royal Opera House Covent Garden, a year after its premiere at La Scala in Milan. The opera was conducted by Rafael Kubelik, directed by Margherita Wallmann and designed by Georges Wakhevitch. Joan Sutherland sang the role of Madame Lidoine, the new prioress, in these performances, at which the composer was present.

In 1984 Joan Sutherland sang the same role in a new Australian Opera production of Poulenc's opera. This was conducted by Richard Bonynge, directed by Elijah Moshinsky and designed by John Bury.

Joan Sutherland as Madame Lidoine with Elsie Morison as Blanche de la Force and Jeannette Sinclair as Sister Constance, at the Royal Opera House Covent Garden, London 1958. Photograph by the Sport and General Press Agency.

Joan Sutherland as Madame Lidoine in Dialogues des Carmelites, *Royal Opera House Covent Garden, 1958. Photograph by Houston Rogers.*

Joan Sutherland as Madame Lidoine in The Australian Opera production, Sydney 1984. Photography by Branco Gaica.

DONNA ANNA

SINCE HER first performances of Donna Anna in Mozart's
Don Giovanni in Vancouver in 1958, in a production by Gunther
Rennert designed by Ita Maximowna, Joan Sutherland has sung the role
in major theatres throughout the world. Notable Sutherland
performances of this role have been in Dublin in 1958, Vienna in 1959,
Glyndebourne 1960, Dallas 1960, La Scala Milan 1967, Metropolitan
New York 1967, Boston 1967, Vancouver 1977, New York 1978, and
Melbourne in 1979.

⬤ *Joan Sutherland as Donna
Anna in* Don Giovanni, *Dallas
1960. Photograph by
Franco Zeffirelli.*

◗ *Costume worn by Joan
Sutherland as Donna Anna in*
Don Giovanni, *designed by
Barbara Matera. Photograph by
Greg Weight.*

◖ *Joan Sutherland as Donna
Anna in* Don Giovanni *at the
Metropolitan Opera, New York
1978. Photograph by
Beth Bergman.*

◗ *Joan Sutherland as Donna
Anna in* Don Giovanni *at the
Staatsoper in Vienna, 1959.
Photograph by Fayer & Co.*

LUCIA

UNDOUBTEDLY THE role for which Joan Sutherland is most acclaimed is that of Donizetti's **Lucia di Lammermoor**. Her first performance of Lucia on 17 February 1959 was a triumphant success for her, and the happy collaboration of a group of remarkable talents – Joan herself in supreme vocal form, directed by Franco Zeffirelli, conducted by Tullio Serafin and coached and encouraged by Richard Bonynge. Since that first performance at the Royal Opera House in London in 1959 (after which she was acclaimed as an international star) until her final performance of Lucia in Barcelona in 1988, Lucia has been the role most often sung by Sutherland in theatres throughout the world.

◖ Joan Sutherland with Franco Zeffirelli after a performance of Lucia di Lammermoor. Photograph by Nancy Sorenson.

◗ Costume worn by Joan Sutherland as Lucia in the Act Three Mad Scene, designed by Franco Zeffirelli for the 1959 Covent Garden production. Photograph by Greg Weight.

◀ Costume design by Franco Zeffirelli for Joan Sutherland as Lucia in the Act Three Mad Scene, Royal Opera House Covent Garden, London 1959.

▶ Costume design by Franco Zeffirelli for Joan Sutherland as Lucia in the Act Two Wedding Scene, Royal Opera House Covent Garden, London 1959.

Joan Sutherland with the famous Greek soprano Maria Callas, herself a celebrated Lucia, backstage at Covent Garden, after the dress rehearsal of Lucia di Lammermoor in 1959. Photograph by London News Agency.

Joan Sutherland as Lucia di Lammermoor, in the Wedding Scene, Hamburg 1971. Photograph by Du Vinage.

Joan Sutherland as Lucia in the Mad Scene of Lucia di Lammermoor. The Australian Opera 1986. Photograph by Branco Gaica.

Costume design by Michael Stennett for Joan Sutherland as Lucia, Mad Scene, in The Australian Opera's 1980 production.

Joan Sutherland in the Mad Scene from Lucia di Lammermoor, at the Royal Opera House Covent Garden, London 1959. Photograph by Houston Rogers.

Poster for Lucia di Lammermoor, Royal Opera House Covent Garden, February 1959. These were Joan Sutherland's first performances of one of her most famous roles.

Joan Sutherland as Lucia di Lammermoor at the Royal Opera House Covent Garden, London 1985, twenty six years after her first performance of the role, in the same theatre. Photograph by Clive Barda.

"Lucia di lammermoor" The Australian Opera 1980   Lucia - Joan Sutherland

RODELINDA

LUCIA DI LAMMERMOOR in 1959 made Joan Sutherland one of the world's most sought-after singers. International appearances and recordings began to appear on her engagement schedules, and new roles had to be prepared. Her first new role after Lucia was that of Handel's Rodelinda which she sang with the Handel Opera Society in June 1959. She again sang *Rodelinda* in Holland, at the Holland Festival in 1973. Her debut at La Scala, Milan was as Lucia on 14 April 1961. During the same season, Sutherland also sang the title role in Bellini's *Beatrice di Tenda.*

◗ *Joan Sutherland as Rodelinda at the Holland Festival in 1973, in a production by Tito Capobianco, designed by Jose Varona. Photograph by Particam-Maria Austria.*

◗ *Costume design by Robin Pidcock for Joan Sutherland as Rodelinda, Handel Opera Society, London 1959.*

◗ *Joan Sutherland as Rodelinda, Handel Opera Society, London 1959. Photograph by Houston Rogers.*

◔ *After a performance of* Bellini's Beatrice di Tenda *in Milan, with Dino Dondi as Filippo. Photograph by Publiphoto.*

◗ *After a recital at Australia House London, in June 1959. Left to right: Richard Bonynge, Lady Harrison, Her Royal Highness Princess Alexandra, Joan Sutherland, and Sir Eric Harrison. Photograph by Sport & General Press Agency.*

◖ *Richard Bonynge and Joan Sutherland in Venice, 1960.*

◐ Overleaf Left: *Costume worn by Joan Sutherland as Violetta in* La Traviata, *designed by Michael Stennett for The Australian Opera performances, 1979 and 1981. Photograph by Greg Weight.*

◑ Overleaf Right: *Costume designed by Franco Zeffirelli and worn by Joan Sutherland as Violetta in* La Traviata, *at the Royal Opera House Covent Garden, London 1960. Photograph by Greg Weight.*

VIOLETTA

FIRST LONDON appearances by Joan Sutherland as Violetta Valery in *La Traviata*, Verdi's Lady of the Camellias, were in 1960. She was ill and unhappy in an undistinguished old production, and the debut was not a success – a bad bout of tracheitis forced the cancellation of the second performance. When fully recovered she resumed the role and enjoyed a considerable success. Since that time Violetta has become one of the great Sutherland interpretations.

🌑 *Joan Sutherland as Violetta in the Luchino Visconti production of* La Traviata *at Covent Garden in 1975. Photograph by Stuart Robinson.*

🌒 *Act One of* La Traviata *at the Royal Opera House, Covent Garden, in 1960: Joan Sutherland with Ronald Lewis and the Australian soprano Marie Collier, who sang Flora. Photograph by Houston Rogers.*

🌓 *Joan Sutherland as Violetta in Act Two Scene Two of Verdi's* La Traviata, *London 1960. Photograph by Houston Rogers.*

🌔 *Costume design by Michael Stennett for Joan Sutherland as Violetta in Act Two Scene Two of* La Traviata, *in The Australian Opera production directed by John Copley.*

🌕 *Costume design by Michael Stennett for Joan Sutherland as Violetta in Act Three of* La Traviata.

🌖 *Joan Sutherland as Violetta in Act Three of* La Traviata, *Melbourne 1979. Photograph by Branco Gaica.*

ELVIRA

BELLINI'S ELVIRA in *I Puritani* was sung by Joan Sutherland for the first time on 24 May 1960 at the Glyndebourne Festival, in a production conducted by Vittorio Gui, directed by Franco Enriquez and designed by Desmond Heeley. This production was subsequently performed at the Edinburgh Festival. In 1961 the Lucia team: Tullio Serafin as conductor; Franco Zeffirelli as director and designer; and Joan Sutherland were reunited in a new production of *I Puritani* in Palermo. This production was seen in Genoa and in London in 1964. Joan Sutherland's Elvira has also been acclaimed in Barcelona, Philadelphia, Boston, San Francisco, New York, Sydney and Stockholm.

✦ *The great Italian conductor Tullio Serafin with Richard Bonynge, Palermo 1961. Photograph by Scafidi.*

◗ *The Mad Scene of* I Puritani *at the Royal Opera House Covent Garden, London 1964, with Joan Sutherland as Elvira and Gabriel Bacquier as Riccardo. Photograph by Donald Southern.*

◗ *Joan Sutherland as Elvira in* I Puritani *at Covent Garden, London 1964. Photograph by Houston Rogers.*

◗ *Break during rehearsals of Bellini's* I Puritani *in 1961: Franco Zeffirelli, the director and designer; Tullio Serafin; Joan Sutherland and Gianni Raimondi, who sang Arturo. Photograph by Scafidi.*

Costume designed by Franco Zeffirelli and worn by Joan Sutherland as Violetta, at the Royal Opera House Covent Garden, London 1960. Photograph by Greg Weight.

Costume design by Michael Stennett for Joan Sutherland as Elvira and Anson Austin as Arturo in the Wedding Scene of I Puritani, The Australian Opera, 1985.

Costume design by Michael Stennett for Joan Sutherland as Elvira in the I Puritani Mad Scene, The Australian Opera, 1985.

AMINA

THE ROYAL Opera House, Covent Garden mounted a new production of Bellini's **La Sonnambula** for Joan Sutherland on 19 October 1960. Tullio Serafin was again the conductor for the premiere, and the opera was directed by Enrico Medioli and designed by Fillipo Sanjust.

In 1962 Joan Sutherland sang Amina at La Scala Milan, in the famous production directed by Luchino Visconti and designed by Piero Tosi. Joan Sutherland's Amina has also been heard in New York, Philadelphia (in concert), Melbourne, Sydney, San Francisco and Los Angeles.

⬤ *Joan Sutherland as Amina in Bellini's* La Sonnambula, *at the Royal Opera House Covent Garden, London 1961. Photograph by Houston Rogers.*

◉ *Joan Sutherland as Amina in Luchino Visconti's production of* La Sonnambula *at La Scala Milan, 1962. Photograph by Erio Piccagliani.*

◐ La Sonnambula *at La Scala Milan 1962, with Joan Sutherland as Amina and Alfredo Kraus as Elvino. Photograph by Erio Piccagliani.*

AMERICA

ALCINA WAS Joan Sutherland's first role in the United States of America, the debut being in Dallas, Texas on 16 November 1960. In subsequent years she has sung in opera and concert throughout the United States, making her debuts with the Lyric Opera of Chicago and the San Francisco Opera in 1961 and her debut with the Metropolitan Opera New York later in the same year. Sutherland was acclaimed by both the public, and the leading singers of the world, past and present. In 1961, Joan Sutherland met Amelita Galli-Curci in California, and having admired Galli-Curci's recordings since childhood remained a firm friend until the singer's death.

In 1962 Joan Sutherland returned to Covent Garden as The Queen of Night in a new production of **Die Zauberflöte** conducted and directed by Otto Klemperer.

On 25 January 1962 Richard Bonynge made his debut as a conductor in concert at the Teatro Eliseo in Rome.

▶ *Card to Joan Sutherland from Hardy Amies, on the occasion of her first performance of the Queen of the Night in* Die Zauberflöte, *1962.*

▶ *Joan Sutherland as the Queen of the Night in* Die Zauberflöte *at the Royal Opera House Covent Garden, January 1962. Photograph by Houston Rogers.*

◀ *Poster from Teatro Eliseo Rome 25 January 1962 on the occasion of Richard Bonynge's debut as a conductor, in a concert at which Joan Sutherland was the soloist.*

◀ *Joan Sutherland with the famous Italian coloratura soprano Amelita Galli-Curci, California 1961.*

◀ *Western Union Telegram to Joan Sutherland from Amelita Galli-Curci, 31 December 1961. Galli-Curci was acclaimed in Europe and America and was a popular recording artist. Her most famous roles were Dinorah (Meyerbeer), Violetta in* La Traviata *(Verdi), Gilda in* Rigoletto *(Verdi), Amina in* La Sonnambula *(Bellini), Lucia di Lammermoor (Donizetti), Rosina in* Il Barbiere di Siviglia *(Rossini) and Norina in* Don Pasquale *(Donizetti).*

▼ *Swedish soprano Birgit Nilsson with Joan Sutherland, at a party after Joan Sutherland's debut at the Metropolitan Opera New York, in 1961. Photograph by Eleanor Morrison.*

To the Queen of Song, as the Queen of the night, with all good wishes, from the Queen's Dressmaker.

WESTERN UNION
TELEGRAM

Teatro Eliseo

ACCADEMIA FILARMONICA
ROMANA

Direttore artistico: MASSIMO BOGIANCKINO

STAGIONE 1961-1962

Giovedì 25 Gennaio - ore 21,15

CONCERTO
DEL
SOPRANO

Joan Sutherland

PROGRAMMA

HAENDEL - Water Music Suite
 - Suite di danze dall'Alcina
 - "Ah, Ruggero crudel..."
   scena e aria dal II. atto dell'Alcina

BELLINI - "Qui la voce sua soave"
   scena e aria dei Puritani

OFFENBACH - Ouverture da La Belle Hélène

THOMAS - "A vos jeux, mes amies..."
   scena della pazzia de Hamlet

Orchestra diretta da
RICHARD BONYNGE

PREZZI
PLATEA L. 5.000   1. GALLERIA esaurito in abb.
BALCONATA L. 3.000   2. GALLERIA L. 1.900

MARGUERITE DE VALOIS

RETURNING TO La Scala Milan in 1962, Joan Sutherland performed
the role of Marguerite de Valois in Meyerbeer's **Les Huguenots**, sung
in Italian as **Gli Ugonotti**. A star cast had been assembled, including
Giulietta Simionato as Valentine, Fiorenza Cossotto as Urbain, Franco
Corelli as Raoul, Vladimiro Ganzarolli as de Nevers, Nicolai Ghiaurov as
Marcel and Giorgio Tozzi as St Bris. The conductor was Gianandrea
Gavazzeni and the director Franco Enriquez. Maria Callas, who was
originally announced to sing the role of Valentine, attended the dress
rehearsal and came backstage to congratulate Joan Sutherland.

In 1968 Joan Sutherland again sang in **Les Huguenots** in concert
performances in London conducted by Richard Bonynge.

In 1981 The Australian Opera mounted a new production of
Les Huguenots conducted by Richard Bonynge directed by Lotfi
Mansouri and designed by Michael Stennett and John Stoddart.

◑ *Joan Sutherland as
Marguerite de Valois in* Les
Huguenots, *Milan 1962.
Photograph by Erio Piccagliani.*

◐ *Joan Sutherland as
Marguerite de Valois in* Les
Huguenots, *Sydney 1981.
Photograph by Branco Gaica.*

◓ *Costume design by Michael
Stennett for Joan Sutherland as
Marguerite de Valois, The
Australian Opera 1981.*

◒ *Letter to Joan Sutherland
from Maria Callas.*

◑ *Joan Sutherland and Maria
Callas backstage during the
dress rehearsal of* Les
Huguenots *at La Scala
Milan 1962.*

◐ *Rehearsal photograph for*
Les Huguenots *in Milan
in 1962, with the famous
Italian tenor Franco Corelli,
Joan Sutherland and the
Italian mezzo-soprano
Fiorenza Cossotto.
Photograph by Farabola.*

SAVOY HOTEL
TELEPHONE TEMPLE BAR 4343
LONDON W C 2

Dear Joan –
Thank you very
dearly for your cable
I remember you
with great affection
and follow your
career with even
greater affection –
Yours
Maria

SEMIRAMIDE

GIOACCHINO ROSSINI'S *Semiramide* was revived for Joan Sutherland in a new production at La Scala Milan in December 1962. The opera was conducted by Gabriele Santini, directed by Margherita Wallmann and designed by Nicola Benois.

In subsequent seasons Joan Sutherland has sung Semiramide in Los Angeles, New York (concert performances), Boston, Sydney, Melbourne and London (concert performances).

In 1968 Joan Sutherland sang Semiramide in a new production of the opera at the Maggio Musicale in Florence, conducted by Richard Bonynge and directed by Sandro Sequi. This production was also seen in Chicago in 1971. In 1983 The Australian Opera presented *Semiramide* in Sydney with Joan Sutherland in a production conducted by Richard Bonynge and directed by Moffatt Oxenbould.

⬩ *Joan Sutherland as Semiramide at La Scala Milan, 1962. Photograph by Erio Piccagliani.*

⬩ *Sketches by Louis Kahan of Joan Sutherland as Semiramide, Melbourne 1965.*

⬩ *Joan Sutherland as Semiramide, Maggio Musicale, Florence 1968. Photograph by Marchiori.*

⬩ *Joan Sutherland as Semiramide with Bruce Martin as Assur, in The Australian Opera production of* Semiramide *in Sydney, 1983. Photograph by Branco Gaica.*

CLEOPATRA

EARLY IN 1963, Joan Sutherland sang for President John F. Kennedy at his Second Inaugural Anniversary Salute in Washington DC. As well as maintaining her heavy recording schedule, she made appearances on television programmes in the United States and in London for Australian television. In June 1963 Joan Sutherland sang again for the Handel Opera Society in London as Handel's Cleopatra in **Giulio Cesare**, conducted by Charles Farncombe, directed by Norman Ayrton and designed by Michael Warre. She was to sing Cleopatra again in 1969 and 1971 in Hamburg in a production conducted by Richard Bonynge, directed by Tito Capobianco and designed by Jose Varona.

◐ *Ella Fitzgerald, Dinah Shore and Joan Sutherland on the Dinah Shore Show, 1963.*

◑ *Richard Bonynge in New York c. 1963. Photograph by Arthur Todd.*

◐ *Joan Sutherland in the garden of Villa San Michele in Fiesole, during the recording of La Sonnambula in 1963.*

◑ *Letter to Joan Sutherland from the violin virtuoso, Yehudi Menuhin, 27 June 1963.*

◐ *Joan, Adam and Richard Bonynge in New York, 1964.*

2, The Grove,
Highgate Village,
London, N.6.
27th June 1963

Miss Joan Sutherland

Dear Miss Sutherland

You transported me last night: I have never heard such
beautiful singing - your voice would be the dream of any
string player, as in addition to the most wonderful
articulation each note seemed to carry a warm weight as
it were, as if your bow arm was drawing the sound out of
the vocal chords in a way which makes me feel both
inspired and discouraged at the same time.

I came backstage hoping to express some of my feelings
at least, but as Princess Margaret was due back and there
were so many formalities I left the message with Ronald
Anderson, hoping that at some future date I might have a
more propitious occasion to speak to you.

Sincerely yours

Yehudi Menuhin

"Julius Caesar" Haendel - Hamburg Opera. 1969

🔴 Joan Sutherland as
Cleopatra, in Giulio Cesare,
Hamburg 1969. Photograph by
Du Vinage.

🔵 Costume design by Jose
Varona for Joan Sutherland as
Cleopatra, in Giulio Cesare,
Hamburg 1969.

🔵 Costume design by Jose
Varona for Joan Sutherland as
Cleopatra, in Giulio Cesare,
Hamburg 1969.

NORMA

PERHAPS THE most challenging of the *bel canto* soprano roles is Bellini's Norma. Since her first assumption of the role in Vancouver in 1963 Norma has become one of Joan Sutherland's most performed and most acclaimed roles.

NORMA.

IF POSSIBLE, THE BLACK VEIL SHOULD REACH THE FLOOR ALL ROUND.

BRONZE, GOLD + SILVER — TO LOOK ENCRUSTED, + HAVE AN 'ANTIQUE' SURFACE

SLIGHTLY STIFFENED HEM

with great admiration — Desmond

◐ *Ronald Stevens as Pollione with Joan Sutherland as Norma, The Australian Opera, 1978. Photograph by Branco Gaica.*

◑ *Joan Sutherland as Norma with Horst Hoffmann as Pollione, The Australian Opera, 1985. Photograph by Branco Gaica.*

◐ *Joan Sutherland as Norma in Vancouver 1963.*

◐ *Joan Sutherland as Norma, The Australian Opera, 1978. Photograph by Branco Gaica.*

◐ *Costume design by Pier Luigi Pizzi for Joan Sutherland as Norma, Act Four, for the Covent Garden production, London 1967.*

◐ *Norma costume design by Desmond Heeley, Metropolitan Opera New York 1970.*

NOEL COWARD

NOEL COWARD was a special friend of both Joan and Richard Bonynge, and they became neighbours when the Bonynge family moved from London to Les Avants in Switzerland in 1969. In 1966 Joan Sutherland and Noël Coward recorded an album of Coward songs, which had been planned a year earlier when on holiday in Jamaica.

On 15 February 1965 Joan Sutherland sang for the first time with Luciano Pavarotti in performances of *Lucia di Lammermoor* in Florida, and in March she sang her first performances of the role of Marguerite in Gounod's *Faust*, prior to performances of *Lucia* and *La Sonnambula* in London, which were the first performances conducted by Richard Bonynge at the Royal Opera House.

◐ *Joan Sutherland's first appearance with tenor Luciano Pavarotti in Miami Florida, in* Lucia di Lammermoor, *in which Pavarotti sang Edgardo. Photograph by John Pineda.*

◑ *Joan Sutherland and Noël Coward at the time of recording their Noël Coward Songs album in 1966. Photograph by Angus McBean.*

◔ *Card to Joan Sutherland from Noël Coward.*

◕ *Joan Sutherland with Noël Coward at the piano, on holiday in Jamaica 1965.*

NOËL COWARD

Just get out there and sing and
dint muck about.
x x + +
love
Noël

HOME SWEET HOME

MELBOURNE WAS the venue for the first performance of the
Sutherland-Williamson International Grand Opera Company on
10 July 1965. The season closed in Brisbane on 16 October in the same
year. The company performed in Melbourne, Adelaide, Sydney and
Brisbane and had a repertoire of seven operas – ***Lucia di Lammermoor,
Eugene Onegin, La Traviata, L'Elisir d'Amore, Semiramide,
La Sonnambula*** and ***Faust***.

The company was the dream of Sir Frank Tait, the last of the four
Tait brothers who headed J.C. Williamson's Theatres. Sir Frank intended
this season to be the highlight of his career, greater than the earlier
Melba-Williamson Opera seasons which the "firm" had also presented.
The dream was realised in terms of audience appreciation and critical
acclaim, but Sir Frank died after the first five weeks of the season, having
witnessed the entire Melbourne season which concluded with an
extraordinary performance of ***La Sonnambula***. At the end of the
performance, which featured Joan Sutherland and Luciano Pavarotti, the
principal singers of the season joined the cast on stage, which was
covered in streamers and flowers, thrown by the capacity audience. The
audience refused to leave and began to chant 'Home Sweet Home, Home
Sweet Home' until an old upright piano was dragged on stage, and
accompanied by Richard Bonynge, Joan sang the song that all wanted to
hear. They were truly home, and this fourteen-week season made a large
Australian public aware of opera as a great musical entertainment. This
led to the huge growth of audiences for performances given by The
Australian Opera, then known as the Elizabethan Trust Opera
Company, who were partners of J.C. Williamson's Theatres in
presenting the season.

▶ *The principals of the
Sutherland-Williamson
International Grand Opera
Company acknowledge
Melbourne's applause,
14 August 1965, after the final
performance of the season.
Left to right: Robert Allman, Joan
Sutherland, Luciano Pavarotti,
Margreta Elkins, Joy Mammen,
Joseph Ward, John Alexander,
Andre Montal, Richard
Bonynge, Dorothy Cole, William
Weibel, Monica Sinclair, Morag
Beaton, Spriro Malas, Lauris
Elms, Gerald Krug, Norman
Ayrton, Martin Scheepers and
Adelio Zagonara. Photograph
by Allan Studios.*

▶ *Curtain Call after* Lucia di
Lammermoor, *10 July 1965.
Left to right: Andre Montal
(Arturo), Cornelis Opthof
(Enrico), Tonina Dorati, (who
designed all seven operas in the
season), Norman Ayrton
(Director of Productions), Joan
Sutherland, Richard Bonynge,
John Alexander (Edgardo) and
Clifford Grant (Raimondo).
Photograph* The Age,
Melbourne.

◀ *Sir Frank and Lady Tait
with Joan Sutherland and
Richard Bonynge immediately
after the first night of*
Lucia di Lammermoor,
Melbourne 1965.

MICHAEL STENNETT

YOUNG AND then unknown British design student Michael Stennett was introduced to Joan Sutherland in 1966. Afterwards he sent her several designs for costumes of some of the heroines in her repertoire.

Since then, he has designed many productions in which Joan Sutherland has sung, for The Australian Opera, the Royal Opera House Covent Garden, Canadian Opera and many others. He is also a portrait painter of note, and has painted Joan Sutherland in several of her greatest roles.

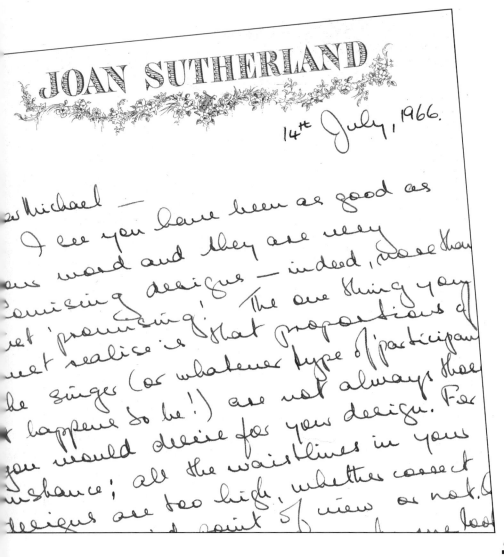

JOAN SUTHERLAND

14th July, 1966.

▶ Costume design by Michael Stennett for Joan Sutherland as Lakmé sent to her in 1966.

◀ Letter from Joan Sutherland to Michael Stennet, acknowledging his designs and saying in part:
'Dear Michael,
I see you have been as good as your word and they are very promising designs – indeed more than just "promising"
...the designs are very beautiful, particularly the Puritani (I see the period paintings have been scrutinised) and the Lakmé certainly has a delicious flavour...
Thank you for sending them to me and keep up the idea of searching into the correct period (also bearing in mind the period of the composer and its influence) and remembering Zeffirelli's (and all designers of his stamp) method of adapting their designs to suit their subject.'

LAKME

HAVING FIRST sung the role of Lakmé in Delibe's opera of the same name in Seattle in 1967, Joan Sutherland repeated her performance in Philadelphia in 1968.

In 1976 The Australian Opera mounted a new production of **Lakmé** for Joan Sutherland, conducted by Richard Bonynge, directed by Norman Ayrton and designed by Desmond Digby. Film Australia made a documentary film of the making of **Lakmé** which revealed the planning, preparation and performance stages of The Australian Opera production.

◑ *Costume worn by Joan Sutherland as Lakmé in Seattle and Philadelphia, designed and made by Barbara Matera. Photograph by Greg Weight.*

◐ *Joan Sutherland as Lakmé, Act Three, Seattle 1967. Photograph by Barry Glass.*

◑ *Costume design by Desmond Digby for Joan Sutherland as Lakmé, The Australian Opera 1976.*

MARIE

A NEW production of Donizetti's comedy, *La Fille du Régiment* was mounted by the Royal Opera House Covent Garden in June 1967. Richard Bonynge conducted the opera, which was directed by Sandro Sequi and designed by Anna Anni and Marcel Escoffier. Joan Sutherland subsequently sang *La Fille du Régiment* in New York, Boston, Cleveland, Atlanta, Memphis, New Orleans, Minneapolis, Detroit, Chicago, Pittsburgh and Sydney.

Joan Sutherland as Marie in La Fille du Régiment *at the Metropolitan Opera in New York, 1972. Photograph by Louis Melancon.*

Joan Sutherland as Marie in La Fille du Régiment, *The Australian Opera 1986. Photograph by Branco Gaica.*

Costume design by Michael Stennett for Joan Sutherland as Marie in La Fille du Régiment, *The Australian Opera 1986.*

Original set design by Henry Bardon for Act One of La Fille du Régiment *for The Australian Opera production in 1986.*

WHO'S AFRAID OF OPERA?

KEEPING UP a busy schedule in the period 1967 to 1972, Joan Sutherland sang frequently in the United States, spending less time in Europe and the United Kingdom. In 1970 she sang in an acclaimed new production of **Norma** at the Metropolitan Opera in New York with Marilyn Horne as Adalgisa.

In 1967 Joan Sutherland sang Euridice in Haydn's **Orfeo ed Euridice** at the Theater an der Wien in Vienna and subsequently at the Edinburgh Festival. These performances were conducted by Richard Bonynge.

Joan Sutherland participated in Gala performances to farewell two great Opera House Directors who had been much involved in her own career, Sir David Webster, who retired from the Royal Opera House, Covent Garden in 1970, and Sir Rudolf Bing, who retired from the Metropolitan Opera in 1972.

In 1972 Richard Bonynge and Joan Sutherland made a television series, 'Who's afraid of opera?', to introduce opera to television viewers. Eight programmes were made, each featuring excerpts from a particular work. Joan sang many of her most celebrated roles, and added three more for the series, Rosina in Rossini's **Il Barbiere di Siviglia**, Offenbach's **La Périchole** and Philine in **Mignon** by Ambroise Thomas.

☞ Joan Sutherland as Euridice in Haydn's Orfeo ed Euridice, *Vienna 1967. Photograph by Gretl Geiger.*

☞ Joan Sutherland and legendary film star Dolores del Rio, New York, 1968.

☞ Joan Sutherland and Richard Bonynge with Placido Domingo and Montserrat Caballé at the Rudolf Bing Gala at the Metropolitan Opera in New York, 22 April 1972. Rudolf Bing was the General Administrator of the Metropolitan Opera between 1950 and 1972.

☞ Sir David Webster, General Administrator of the Royal Opera House, Covent Garden, with Joan Sutherland and Welsh soprano Gwyneth Jones at his Farewell Gala in 1970. Photograph by Evening Standard, London.

☞ Joan Sutherland sings an aria from Crispino e la Comare *on the Bell Telephone Hour on New Year's Day, 1967.*

MARIA STUARDA

DONIZETTI'S OPERA *Maria Stuarda*, based on the last days of Mary Queen of Scots, was sung for the first time by Joan Sutherland at the War Memorial Opera House in San Francisco on 12 November 1971. The production was conducted by Richard Bonynge, directed by Tito Capobianco and designed by Pier Luigi Pizzi. Joan Sutherland's costumes were designed by Jose Varona.

Joan Sutherland's Maria Stuarda has also been heard in Las Palmas in 1975, Holland and London in 1977.

☛ Costume worn by Joan Sutherland as Maria Stuarda, designed by Jose Varona. Photograph by Greg Weight.

◀ Costume design by Jose Varona for Joan Sutherland as Maria Stuarda in 1971, for performances at the San Francisco Opera.

☛ Joan Sutherland as Maria Stuarda, Royal Opera House Covent Garden, 1977. Photograph by Reg Wilson.

LUCREZIA BORGIA

NOTORIOUS MURDERESS Lucrezia Borgia, as created by Donizetti, is one of opera's great *bel canto* heroines. Joan Sutherland sang the role for the first time in Vancouver in 1972, in a production conducted by Richard Bonynge, directed by Irving Guttman and designed by Jose Varona. In 1975 she sang the role again, in Houston, and in 1977 the opera entered The Australian Opera's repertoire in a new production by George Ogilvie, designed by Kristian Fredrikson.

In 1980 Joan Sutherland sang ***Lucrezia Borgia*** in London, at Covent Garden and at the Rome Opera in a production conducted by Richard Bonynge, directed by John Copley and designed by Michael Stennett and John Pascoe. In 1982 Sydney again heard Joan Sutherland in the role, as did Stockholm in a concert performance. In 1989 Joan Sutherland sang the opera in both Barcelona and in Paris.

❦ *Costume worn by Joan Sutherland as Lucrezia Borgia, designed by Jose Varona. Photograph by Greg Weight.*

❦ *Costume design by Jose Varona for Joan Sutherland as Lucrezia Borgia, Act One, Vancouver 1972.*

☛ *Costume design by Kristian Fredrikson for Joan Sutherland as Lucrezia Borgia, Act Three, The Australian Opera 1977.*

☚ *Joan Sutherland as Lucrezia Borgia, The Australian Opera, 1982. Curtain call after Act One, with Lamberto Furlan as Gennaro and Bernadette Cullen as Maffio Orsini. Photograph by Branco Gaica.*

☛ *Costume design by Michael Stennett for Joan Sutherland as Lucrezia Borgia, Act Three, Royal Opera House London, 1980.*

☚ *Costume design by Michael Stennett for Joan Sutherland as Lucrezia Borgia, Act Two, Royal Opera House London, 1980.*

LUCREZIA BORGIA — MISS JOAN SUTHERLAND / ACT III SC II

NEW ROLES

THREE NEW roles for Joan Sutherland during the 1970s were Rosalinde in Johann Strauss' **Die Fledermaus**, Leonora in Verdi's **Il Trovatore** and the title role in **Suor Angelica** by Puccini.

Rosalinde in the Strauss operetta was first heard by Sutherland fans in the San Francisco Opera production of 1973, a production by Lotfi Mansouri conducted by Richard Bonynge. In 1980 Joan Sutherland sang Rosalinde in San Diego in a production by Tito Capobianco featuring Beverley Sills as Adele, and in 1982 the operetta returned to The Australian Opera's repertoire in a new production by Anthony Besch. The Australian Opera production was nationally simulcast and brought forth mountains of fan mail from opera lovers all over the continent who had shared the excitement of a Sutherland performance 'live from the Sydney Opera House'. The operetta was chosen as the Opera in the Park performance in the Sydney Domain in 1983, and Joan Sutherland also sang in further stage performances during January. The Royal Opera House, Covent Garden has invited Joan Sutherland to sing Rosalinde in London in the 1990/91 season.

Leonora was also first sung by Joan Sutherland in San Francisco in 1975 in a production by Patrick Libby. In 1981 Sutherland sang Leonora at Covent Garden in London, and in 1983 for The Australian Opera in Sydney in a production directed by Elijah Moshinsky and designed by Sidney Nolan and Luciana Arrighi. Sidney Nolan created a number of gauzes for The Australian Opera production, those for Leonora's first aria, *'Tacea la notte placida'*, inspired by Sutherland's voice. Joan Sutherland sang in a new production of **Il Trovatore** at the Metopolitan Opera in New York in 1987.

Sutherland sang four performances of **Suor Angelica** in Sydney in 1977, her first Puccini role on the professional stage. The production was directed by Moffatt Oxenbould and designed by Desmond Digby.

🝔 *Joan Sutherland with fan mail received after The Australian Opera/Australian Broadcasting Corporation simulcast of* Die Fledermaus, *in 1982.*

🝔 *Joan Sutherland as Rosalinde in* Die Fledermaus, *San Francisco Opera 1973. Photograph by Carolyn Mason Jones.*

🝔 *Joan Sutherland as Leonora with Jonathan Summers as Di Luna in* Il Trovatore, *The Australian Opera 1983. Photograph by Branco Gaica.*

🝔 *Original design by Australian painter Sidney Nolan, for a scenic gauze for* Il Trovatore *and the heroine Leonora's first aria 'Tacea la notte placida', The Australian Opera 1983.*

🝔 *Joan Sutherland as Suor Angelica in The Australian Opera's production of Puccini's one-act opera 1977.*

ESCLARMONDE

MASSENET WROTE *Esclarmonde* for the American soprano Sybil Sanderson, who sang it for the first time in Paris in 1889. Joan Sutherland sang the role first in San Francisco in 1974 in a production conducted by Richard Bonynge, directed by Lotfi Mansouri and designed by Beni Montresor. Joan's sumptuous costumes were designed and made by Barbara Matera.

In 1976 the production transferred successfully to the Metropolitan Opera in New York, and both Richard Bonynge and Joan Sutherland were acclaimed by critics and the public for reviving a work not heard for nearly forty years.

In 1983 *Esclarmonde*, in the same production, was presented at the Royal Opera House, Covent Garden in London. An Australian Opera production was planned for Sydney in 1985, but a new production of *Norma* staged in the Concert Hall of the Sydney Opera House was substituted. Kenneth Rowell's designs for the proposed *Esclarmonde* were completed, though never realised.

◐ *Joan Sutherland as Esclarmonde, Royal Opera House Covent Garden, 1983. Photograph by Reg Wilson.*

◐ *Costume worn by Joan Sutherland in Act One of* Esclarmonde, *designed by Barbara Matera. Photograph by Greg Weight.*

◐ *Costume design by Barbara Matera for Joan Sutherland as Esclarmonde Act One, San Francisco Opera, 1974.*

◐ *Original design by Kenneth Rowell for Joan Sutherland as Esclarmonde, for a proposed Australian Opera production of the opera in 1985.*

ANNA GLAWARI

FOLLOWING THE success of *Die Fledermaus* in 1973, Joan Sutherland undertook a new Viennese operetta role – that of Anna Glawari, in *The Merry Widow* by Franz Lehar. Her first performances were in 1976 in Vancouver in a new performing version by Richard Bonynge, directed by Lotfi Mansouri. In 1978 and 1979 Sutherland sang *The Merry Widow* in Sydney, Adelaide and Melbourne. Lotfi Mansouri was again the director with designs by Kristian Fredrikson.

In 1981 Joan Sutherland sang Anna Glawari for the first time in the United States with the San Francisco Opera and in 1988, as part of The Australian Opera's Bicentennial Season, Joan Sutherland and Richard Bonynge again performed *The Merry Widow* in gala performances at the Sydney Opera House. In 1989 Joan Sutherland and Richard Bonynge performed the operetta in Dallas, Texas.

🌢 *Joan Sutherland as Anna Glawari in Act Two of* The Merry Widow, *in The Australian Opera production, in 1978. Photograph by William Moseley.*

👁 *Curtain Call after a performance of* The Merry Widow, *San Francisco 1981. Photograph by Ira Nowinski.*

◀ *Richard Bonynge and Joan Sutherland during curtain calls for* The Merry Widow *during The Australian Opera's Bicentennial Season, 1988. Photograph by Branco Gaico.*

🌢 *Poster designed by Jose Varona for the Vancouver Opera, 1976.*

SITA

SINGING HER second Massenet role as Sita, Joan Sutherland performed in *Le Roi de Lahore* in 1977. Richard Bonynge conducted the opera in a production by Sandro Sequi for the Vancouver Opera. The designer was Fiorella Mariani and Joan's costumes were made by Barbara Matera.

◐ *Costume sketch and fabric swatch used by Barbara Matera for a costume for Joan Sutherland in* Le Roi de Lahore.

◑ *Costume sketch by Barbara Matera for a costume for Joan Sutherland in* Le Roi de Lahore.

◑ *Costume sketches by Barbara matera for costumes for Joan Sutherland in* Le Roi de Lahore.

◐ *Original set sketch by Fiorella Mariani for* Le Roi de Lahore, *Temple Scene.*

◑ *Original set sketch by Fiorella Mariani for* Le Roi de Lahore.

◓ *Joan Sutherland as Sita in* Le Roi de Lahore. *Photograph by Philip Clement.*

ELETTRA

WHEN ELETTRA was performed by Joan Sutherland in **Idomeneo**
in 1979, it was her debut in this Mozart role. The Australian Opera's
production, directed by Robin Lovejoy and designed by John Truscott,
was originally created for the Victoria State Opera.

❦ *Costume design by John
Truscott for Joan Sutherland as
Elettra in* Idomeneo, *1979.*

❦ *Joan Sutherland as Elettra
in The Australian Opera's
performances in 1979.
Photograph by Branco Gaica.*

HONOURS

RECEIVING THE award of Commander of the Order of the British Empire in 1961, Joan Sutherland subsequently became a Companion of the Order of Australia in 1975. In the Queen's New Year Honours for 1979, the award DBE made her Dame Joan Sutherland.

In 1980, after a performance of **Lucrezia Borgia** at Covent Garden, Joan Sutherland was presented with the Silver Medal of the Royal Opera House by Sir John Tooley. She was honoured again in 1982 at the Royal Opera House in a Gala Concert on 17 October.

Richard Bonynge was awarded the Commander of the Order of the British Empire in 1977 and made an Officer of the Order of Australia in 1984.

In 1989 France honoured both Joan Sutherland and Richard Bonynge who were created *Commandeurs des arts et des lettres* for their services to French music.

▶ *Joan Sutherland receiving the Royal Opera House Silver Medal for Long Service from Sir John Tooley after a performance of* Lucrezia Borgia *in 1980. Photograph by Reg Wilson.*

▶ *Joan Sutherland and Her Majesty, the Queen Mother, after a performance of* Lucrezia Borgia *at Covent Garden in 1980. Photograph by Donald Southern.*

▶ *Gala Concert in the Concert Hall of the Sydney Opera House, 23 January 1983: Richard Bonynge, Joan Sutherland and Luciano Pavarotti. Photograph by Branco Gaica.*

▶ *Joan Sutherland, His Royal Highness the Prince of Wales and Dame Edna Everage (Barry Humphries) at the Inaugural Gala Concert for the Australian Music Foundation in London. Photograph by United Press International.*

▶ *Joan Sutherland with young fans after the 1984 Esso Opera in the Park performance of* Lucia di Lammermoor *presented by The Australian Opera in the Sydney Domain.*

▼ *Marilyn Horne, Joan Sutherland and Luciano Pavarotti in a Live from Lincoln Center concert in New York, 1981. Photograph by Louis Peres.*

HEROINES

DURING THE 1980s Joan Sutherland added four roles to her repertoire. Amalia the heroine of Verdi's *I Masnadieri* in 1980, Cilea's **Adriana Lecouvreur** in 1983, Donizetti's **Anna Bolena** in 1984 and Ophélie, the heroine of **Hamlet** by Thomas in 1985.

I Masnadieri was presented by The Australian Opera in a production directed by Peter Beauvais designed by Allan Lees and Michael Stennett. In 1984 Joan Sutherland again sang Amalia, in San Diego in a production by Tito Capobianco.

Sutherland's Adriana Lecouvreur was heard in San Diego in 1983, in Sydney in 1984 and in Toronto in 1988. In San Diego, the opera was directed by Tito Capobianco, and in Sydney and Toronto by John Copley.

Anna Bolena, another of the greatest of the *bel canto* heroines was first sung by Joan Sutherland with The Canadian Opera Company in Toronto, in a production by Lotfi Mansouri, designed by John Pascoe and Michael Stennett. This production was subsequently given in Detroit, San Francisco, Chicago and Houston. The Royal Opera House, Covent Garden mounted a new production of the opera for Joan Sutherland in London in 1988, directed and designed by John Pascoe.

Joan Sutherland sang Ophélie in Toronto in 1985 in Lotfi Mansouri's production of the Thomas opera.

◢ *Joan Sutherland as Ophélie, in the* Hamlet *Mad Scene, Toronto 1985. Photograph by Gary Beechey.*

◀ *Joan Sutherland as Adriana Lecouvreur with Anson Austin as Maurizio, The Australian Opera 1984. Photograph by Branco Gaica.*

◥ *Costume design by Michael Stennett for Joan Sutherland in Act One of* Adriana Lecouvreur, *1983.*

▶ *Joan Sutherland as Anna Bolena, Royal Opera House, Covent Garden, London 1988. Photograph by Clive Barda.*

▼ *Clifford Grant as Massimiliano and Joan Sutherland as Amalia in* I Masnadieri, *Sydney 1980. Photograph by Branco Gaica.*

Adriana Lecouvreur.
Adriana as Roxane Act I. Dame Joan Sutherland.

FAREWELLS

JOAN SUTHERLAND has announced that she will give her last staged operatic performances in March 1991, singing one of her earliest roles, Countess Almaviva in **Le Nozze de Figaro**, in Barcelona as part of the commemoration of the two hundreth anniversary of Mozart's death. In September 1990 she will sing her final staged performances for The Australian Opera, as Marguerite de Valois in **Les Huguenots**, in the Sydney Opera House.

These performances will give audiences the opportunity to honour a great lady, and to salute a remarkable career.

Dame Joan Sutherland. Photograph by V. Tony Hauser.

Curtain call on the stage of the Royal Opera House, Covent Garden at the 1988 Gala to honour Sir John Tooley on his retirement as General Administrator. Photograph by Zoë Dominic.

STAGE REPERTOIRE

By Francesco Cilea (1866-1950)   Text by Arturo Colautti
First performed in Milan, 1902

   Based on the life of the French tragedienne, Adrienne Lecouvreur, who lived from 1692 to 1730. Adriana is poisoned by her noble rival for the love of Maurizio, the Count of Saxony. Joan Sutherland first sang the role of Adriana in San Diego in 1983.

Adriana Lecouvreur

By Giuseppe Verdi (1813-1901)   Text by Antonio Ghislanzoni
First performed in Cairo, 1871

   Set in ancient Egypt, Aida is a captive Ethiopian princess who is loved by Radames, leader of the Egyptian army. He in turn is loved by Amneris, daughter of Pharaoh. Aida is urged by her warrior father to persuade Radames to betray his country and when he is condemned to death, she joins him in the dungeon which becomes their tomb. Joan Sutherland sang two roles in *Aida* during her time as a member of the company of the Royal Opera House Covent Garden – the offstage Priestess for the first time in 1952 in London, and the title role, also in London, in 1954.

Aida

By George Frideric Handel (1685-1759)   Text by Antonio Marchi
First performed in London, 1735

   The story is taken from Ariosto's *Orlando Furioso* and tells of the enchantress Alcina, whose Kingdom is a magic island to which she lures noble warriors, transforming them into animals, plants and rocks after she has tired of them. Her power is lost in confrontation with the knight Ruggiero and his bride Bradamante, who has followed him to Alcina's realm. Joan Sutherland first sang the role of Alcina in 1957 in London, for the Handel Opera Society.

Alcina

By Gaetano Donizetti (1797-1848)   Text by Felice Romani
First performed in Milan, 1830

   One of Donizetti's operas based on sixteenth century historical figures. Anna Bolena (Anne Boleyn) is the Queen of Enrico (Henry VIII), who has tired of her and is in love with Giovanna (Jane Seymour). Anna is condemned to death and the opera ends with a dramatic denunication of her husband and his new bride. Joan Sutherland's first performances of Anna Bolena were in Toronto in 1984.

Anna Bolena

By Giuseppe Verdi (1813-1901)   Text by Antonio Somma
First performed in Rome, 1859

   The opera exists in two settings, the Swedish Court of Gustavus III or Boston in the latter part of the seventeenth century. Gustavus (or Riccardo, Governor of Boston) loves Amelia, the wife of his secretary and friend Anckarstroom (or Renato), who discovers the situation and joins in a plot which leads to the assassination of Gustavus. Amelia was Joan Sutherland's first prima donna role at Covent Garden, London, in 1952, when she substituted for an indisposed colleague.

Un Ballo in Maschera
A Masked Ball

By Vincenzo Bellini (1802-1835)   Text by Felice Romani
First performed in Venice, 1833

   Set in fifteenth century Milan, the opera tells of the tragedy of the Duchess Beatrice, rejected and ultimately condemned to death by her husband, Filippo Visconti. Joan Sutherland first sang Beatrice di Tenda at La Scala Milan in April 1961, having sung the opera in concert performance in New York in the previous month.

Beatrice di Tenda

By Georges Bizet (1838-1875)   Text by Henri Meilhac and Ludovic Halévy
First performed in Paris, 1875

   Based on the novella of Prosper Merimée, the opera tells of the gypsy Carmen and her entanglement with Don José, a soldier who deserts the army and his village sweetheart Micaela, for Carmen who eventually leaves him for the toreador Escamillo. Carmen meets her death at the hands of the obsessed Don José. Joan Sutherland performed two roles in *Carmen* while a member of the Royal Opera at Covent Garden: Frasquita, one of

Carmen

Carmen's two friends, for the first time in 1953, in London; and Micaela in 1955, also in London.

Les Contes d'Hoffmann
The Tales of Hoffmann

By Jacques Offenbach (1819-1880)   Text by Jules Barbier and Michel Carré
First performed in Paris, 1881

Offenbach died during the rehearsals of **Les Contes d'Hoffmann** and since that time various editors have made versions and different sequences of the acts, for stage performances. The opera tells of the poet Hoffmann and his recollections in a student tavern of his three past loves: the doll Olympia, the courtesan Giulietta and the pure Antonia. Each love is thwarted by the intervention of an evil figure, who is also present listening to Hoffmann's tales and who takes from him Stella, his current love, who embodies the qualities of all three former passions. Joan Sutherland sang Antonia for the first time in 1954 in London, Giulietta in 1955 in Glasgow and Olympia in 1955 in London. In 1970 in Seattle, she sang all four soprano roles – Olympia, Giulietta, Antonia and Stella – in Richard Bonynge's performing version of Offenbach's opera.

Dialogues des Carmelites
The Dialogues of the Carmelites

By Francis Poulenc (1897-1963)   Text by Georges Bernanos
First performed in Milan, 1957

Set in revolutionary France, the opera tells of the Carmelite nuns of Compiègne, who go to the guillotine in defiance of the decree forbidding the religious to live in communities. Joan Sutherland sang the role of Madame Lidoine, the new prioress, Mother Marie of Saint Augustine, for the first time in London in 1958.

Don Giovanni

By Wolfgang Amadeus Mozart (1756-1791)   Text by Lorenzo da Ponte
First performed in Prague, 1787

A version of the Don Juan legend telling of the last days of the libertine Don Giovanni, pursued both on earth and from the grave, by those he has wronged during his dissolute life. Joan Sutherland first sang the dramatic role of Donna Anna in **Don Giovanni** in 1958 in Vancouver.

Elektra

By Richard Strauss (1864-1949)   Text by Hugo von Hofmannsthal
First performed in Dresden, 1909

Based on Sophocles' version of the Oresteia, the opera tells of Elektra, daughter of Agamemnon, murdered by his wife Clytemnestra, and the vengeance of Elektra and her brother Orestes. While a member of the company of the Royal Opera House at Covent Garden, Joan Sutherland sang the role of the Overseer in **Elektra**, for the first time in 1953.

Esclarmonde

By Jules Massenet (1840-1912)   Text by Alfred Blau and Louis de Gramont
First performed in Paris, 1889

The love story of the knight Roland and the enchantress Esclarmonde, daughter of the Emperor Phorcas of Byzantium. Joan Sutherland gave her first performances of **Esclarmonde** in 1974 in San Francisco.

Faust

By Charles Gounod (1818-1893)   Text by Jules Barbier and Michel Carré
First performed in Paris, 1859

A version of the story of Faust, the old philosopher who sells his soul to Mephistopheles, in return for eternal youth and the promise of the virtuous Marguerite. She is eventually abandoned by Faust and condemned to death for killing the child she has borne him. Joan Sutherland sang Marguerite for the first time in 1965, in Philadelphia.

La Fille du Régiment
The Daughter of the Regiment

By Gaetano Donizetti (1797-1848)   Text by Jules H. Vernoy de St-Georges and Jean Francois Bayard
First performed in Paris, 1840

The story of Marie, presumed to be an abandoned orphan, who is brought up by a French regiment. The opera tells of her love for Tonio, a Tyrolean peasant and her entry into society when she is reunited with her aunt, the Marquise de Birkenfeld. Joan Sutherland first sang Marie in 1966, in London.

Die Fledermaus
The Bat

By Johann Strauss (1825-1899)   Text by Carl Haffner and Richard Genée
First performed in Vienna, 1874

A comedy of marital infidelity, masquerade and intrigue in nineteenth century Vienna, involving Gabriel von Eisenstein and his wife Rosalinde. Joan Sutherland sang Rosalinde for the first time in 1973, in San Francisco.

Der Freischütz
The Freeshooter

By Carl Maria von Weber (1786-1826)   Text by Friedrich Kind
First performed in Berlin, 1821

Set in Bohemia in the eighteenth century, the opera tells of the young huntsman Max, who makes a pact with the evil Kaspar, to forge magic bullets in order to win the hand of Agathe, who will wed the winner of a shooting contest. Joan Sutherland sang Agathe while a member of the Royal Opera at Covent Garden in 1954, in London.

Giulio Cesare
Julius Caesar

By George Frideric Handel (1685-1759)   Text by Nicola Francesco Haym
First performed in London, 1724

Based on Julius Caesar's experiences in Egypt with Cleopatra in 48 BC. Joan Sutherland first sang the role of Cleopatra in 1963, in London.

Gloriana

By Benjamin Britten (1913-1976)   Text by William Plomer
First performed in London, 1953

The opera was first performed in connection with the coronation of Queen Elizabeth II in 1953 and tells of Gloriana, Elizabeth I, and the latter years of her reign, especially her relationship with Robert Devereux, Earl of Essex. Joan Sutherland was the second artist to sing the role of Lady Penelope Rich in *Gloriana* in 1953, the first being the British soprano, Jennifer Vyvyan.

Hamlet

By Ambroise Thomas (1811-1896)   Text by Jules Barbier and Michel Carré
First performed in Paris, 1868

Thomas' version of Shakespeare's tragedy has provided Joan Sutherland with her final planned stage role, Ophélie, which she sang for the first time in 1985, in Toronto.

Les Huguenots
The Huguenots

By Giacomo Meyerbeer (1791-1864)   Text by Eugene Scribe and Emile Deschamps
First performed in Paris, 1836

Set in France in 1592, the opera tells of the events leading up to the massacre of the protestant Huguenots on Saint Bartholemew's Eve. Joan Sutherland first sang the role of Queen Marguerite de Valois in *Les Huguenots* at La Scala Milan, in 1962.

Idomeneo, re di Creta
Idomeneo, King of Crete

By Wolfgang Amadeus Mozart (1756-1791)   Text by Giambattista Varesco
First performed in Munich, 1781

A story of Idomeneo, King of Crete, who has promised Neptune that if he and his followers survive a shipwreck, he will sacrifice the first living thing he sees on land: this is his son, Idamante. The role of the jealous Elettra was sung by Joan Sutherland in Sydney, in 1979.

Judith

By Eugene Goossens (1893-1962)   Text by Arnold Bennett
First performed in London, 1929

Based on the Old Testament story of Judith's slaying of Holofernes. Goossens' opera gave Joan Sutherland her first stage role at the New South Wales State Conservatorium of Music in 1951, in Sydney.

Lakmé

By Léo Delibes (1836-1891)   Text by Edmond Gondinet and Philippe Gille
First performed in Paris, 1883

The opera is set in British India in the mid nineteenth century and tells of Lakmé, the daughter of a fanatical Brahmin priest, and her forbidden love for Gerald, a British officer. Lakmé, eventually realising that Gerald's sense of duty to his country will force him to leave her, suicides by eating the flowers of the poisonous datura plant. Joan Sutherland first sang the role of Lakmé in 1967, in Seattle.

Lucia di Lammermoor

By Gaetano Donizetti (1797-1848)   Text by Salvatore Cammarano
First performed in Naples, 1835

Based on Sir Walter Scott's novel, *The Bride of Lammermoor*, the opera tells of Lucia, the daughter of an impoverished noble family, who is forced into an arranged marriage, thus forsaking her true love, Edgardo. On her wedding night, Lucia returns to the nuptial feast, after losing her reason and murdering her bridegroom. Joan Sutherland's first performances of Lucia at the Royal Opera House Covent Garden in February 1959 made her an international star.

Lucrezia Borgia

By Gaetano Donizetti (1797-1848)   Text by Felice Romani
First performed in Milan, 1833
Set in sixteenth century Venice and Ferrara, the opera tells of the notorious Lucrezia Borgia, a known murderess, who unwittingly poisons her own son, Gennaro. The role of Lucrezia was first sung by Joan Sutherland in 1972, in Vancouver.

Maria Stuarda

By Gaetano Donizetti (1797-1848)   Text by Felice Romani
First performed in Naples, 1834 as **Buondelmonte** in Milan, 1835 as **Maria Stuarda**.
Another of Donizetti's operas based on British history, telling of the captivity and eventual execution of Mary Stuart, Queen of Scots. Joan Sutherland's first performances of the title role in **Maria Stuarda** were in 1971, in San Francisco.

I Masnadieri
The Robbers

By Giuseppie Verdi (1813-1901)   Text by Andrea Maffei
First performed in London, 1847
I Masnadieri was based on Schiller's play **The Robbers** and was written for the Swedish soprano Jenny Lind. It tells of the rivalry between two brothers, their love for the same woman, and the unhappy life of Carlo, the elder brother who is forced into banditry. Joan Sutherland sang the role of Amalia in **I Masnadieri** for the first time in 1980, in Sydney.

Die Meistersinger von Nürnberg
The Mastersingers of Nuremberg

By Richard Wagner (1813-1883)
First performed in Munich, 1868
Set in Nuremberg in the sixteenth century, the opera tells of the Mastersingers, the Masters' Guilds and the attempts of Walther von Stolzing to win the hand of Eva Pogner, the prize in a contest for a master song. Joan Sutherland sang Eva in a new production of the opera at the Royal Opera House in 1957, in London.

The Merry Widow

By Franz Lehar (1870-1948)   Text by Viktor Leon and Leo Stein
First performed in Vienna, 1905
The operetta tells of Anna Glawari, a rich widow, and the plot of the Pontevedrian Ambassador to retain her fortune in the National Bank of his impoverished country. Anna meets her former sweetheart, Danilo, who had abandoned her when she was poor and unknown. Joan Sutherland first sang Anna Glawari in 1976, in Vancouver.

The Midsummer Marriage

By Michael Tippett (born 1905)
First performed in London, 1955
The Midsummer Marriage is described by Tippett as a 'quest' opera, not unlike **Die Zauberflöte**. Mark and Jenifer seek for truth and a deeper understanding and knowledge of each other. Joan Sutherland sang the role of Jenifer in the world premiere of the opera in 1955, in London.

Norma

By Vincenzo Bellini (1802-1835)   Text by Felice Romani
First performed in Milan, 1831
The opera tells of the Druid priestess Norma's forbidden love for Pollione, a Roman officer, by whom she has borne two children. Although Pollione in turn loves Adalgisa, a young priestess, he and Norma are reunited when burned for their desecration of the law. Joan Sutherland sang the small role of Clotilde in London in 1952, and first sang the title role in Vancouver, in 1963.

Le Nozze di Figaro
The Marriage of Figaro

By Wolfgang Amadeus Mozart (1756-1791)   Text by Lorenzo da Ponte
First performed in Vienna, 1786
Based on the play by Beaumarchais, the opera centres on the household of Count Almaviva, at the time of the marriage of the Count's valet Figaro, to Susanna, the maid of Countess Almaviva. It is a poignant story about folly in love and marriage. Joan Sutherland first sang the role of Countess Almaviva in 1953, in Edinburgh.

By Josef Haydn (1732-1809)   Text by Badini
First performed in Florence, 1951

Orfeo ed Euridice

The opera was commissioned for London in 1791, but not performed in the composer's lifetime. Joan Sutherland sang the role of Euridice for the first time in 1967, in Vienna.

By Giuseppe Verdi (1813-1901)   Text by Arrigo Boito
First performed in Milan, 1887

Otello

Verdi's version of Shakespeare's tragedy, in which Joan Sutherland sang the role of the wronged Desdemona for the first time in 1957, in London.

By Vincenzo Bellini (1802-1835)   Text by Carlo Pepoli
First performed in Paris, 1835

I Puritani
The Puritans

Set in Plymouth at the time of the English Civil War, the opera tells the story of Elvira, daughter of the Puritan Lord Walton, and her love for the Cavalier, Arturo. Joan Sutherland's first performances of the role of Elvira were at the 1960 Glyndebourne Festival.

By Giuseppe Verdi (1813-1901)   Text by Francesco Maria Piave
First performed in Venice, 1851

Rigoletto

Set in Mantua in the sixteenth century, the opera tells the tragic story of Gilda, daughter of the court jester Rigoletto and her love for his dissolute master, the Duke of Mantua. After Gilda is seduced by the Duke, Rigoletto seeks vengeance and arranges for his murder by a paid assassin, but Gilda intervenes and is herself killed, instead of the Duke. Joan Sutherland's first performances of Gilda were in 1957, in London.

By Richard Wagner (1813-1883)   Stage Festival Play for 3 days and a preliminary evening
First complete performance in Bayreuth, 1871

Der Ring des Nibelungen

Wagner's epic tetralogy is a vast and complex version of the German Nibelung legends, in four separate works: *Das Rheingold, Die Walküre, Siegfried* and *Götterdämmerung*. During her time as a member of the company of the Royal Opera House, Covent Garden, Joan Sutherland sang small roles in all four operas: Woglinde in *Das Rheingold* for the first time in 1954, Helmwige in *Die Walküre* for the first time in 1953, the offstage Woodbird in *Siegfried* in 1954 and Woglinde in *Götterdämmerung* in 1954.

By George Frideric Handel (1685-1759)   Text by Antonio Salvi and Francesco Haym
First performed in London, 1725

Rodelinda

A complicated story of intrigue at the court of Lombardy. Rodelinda, the queen, believes her husband Bertarido to be dead and is courted by the usurper Grimoaldo. Bertarido returns disguised and eventually is restored to the throne and his faithful Rodelinda. Joan Sutherland first sang in *Rodelinda* in 1959, in London.

By Giacomo Puccini (1858-1924)   Text by Giovacchino Forzano
First performed in New York, 1918

Suor Angelica
Sister Angelica

One of the three operas which make up Puccini's *Il Trittico*, Suor Angelica is a young princess who has been sent to a convent, having borne an illegitimate son. Her aunt comes to the convent after seven years and tells her that her son is dead. Angelica commits suicide to join him and her sin is pardoned in a miraculous appearance by the Virgin. Joan Sutherland sang the role of Suor Angelica in 1977, in Sydney.

By Giacomo Puccini (1858-1924)   Text by Giuseppe Adami
First performed in New York, 1918

Il Tabarro
The Cloak

The first of the *Il Trittico* operas is set on a barge in the Seine. Michele the barge owner, has a young wife Giorgetta, who is involved in an adulterous affair with the stevedore Luigi. Michele discovers the affair and strangles Luigi, hiding the body under his cloak and eventually revealing the corpse to his distraught wife. The role of Giorgetta was sung by Joan Sutherland while a student at the Royal College of Music, London in 1952.

By Giuseppe Verdi (1813-1901)   Text by Francesco Maria Piave
First performed in Venice, 1853

La Traviata
The Wayward One

Verdi's version of the story of **The Lady of the Camellias**, by Alexandre Dumas the younger, which is in turn based on the life of Alphonsine Duplessis. Violetta, a consumptive courtesan, abandons her wayward life to live with Alfredo, but she is persuaded by Alfredo's father to leave his son, thereby preserving the family's honour. Violetta and Alfredo are reunited as she dies, her sacrifice having been revealed by Alfredo's father. Joan Sutherland first sang Violetta in 1960, in London.

Il Trovatore
The Troubadour

By Giuseppe Verdi (1813-1901)   Text by Salvatore Cammarano
First performed in Rome, 1853

A complicated story concerning the gypsy Azucena and her revenge on the house of di Luna for having burnt her mother as a witch. Joan Sutherland gave her first performances of Leonora, the soprano heroine of *Il Trovatore*, in 1975, in San Francisco.

Die Zauberflöte
The Magic Flute

By Wolfgang Amadeus Mozart (1756-1791)   Text by Emanuel Schikanader
First performed in Vienna, 1791

A fantasy concerning the young prince Tamino and his quest to be worthy of Pamina, the daughter of the Queen of the Night. At different times in her career, Joan Sutherland has sung three different roles in Mozart's opera. In 1952 the role of the First Lady was her first appearance at the Royal Opera House, Covent Garden. With the same company in London, Sutherland sang Pamina for the first time in 1956 and in 1961, again at Covent Garden, she sang the role of the Queen of the Night, in a new production of the opera.

Le Roi de Lahore
The King of Lahore

By Jules Massenet (1842-1912)   Text by Louis Gallet
First performed in London, 1877

Set in ancient India, both King Alim and Scindia love Sita. Scindia kills Alim and Sita commits suicide to join him in Paradise. Sita was Joan Sutherland's second Massenet role, which she sang for the first time in 1977, in Vancouver.

Samson

By George Frideric Handel (1685-1759)   Text from the poetry of John Milton
First performed in London, 1743

Handel's oratorio is occasionally staged, and tells the Old Testament story of Samson. Joan Sutherland sang the role of the Israelite Woman on stage with the Royal Opera in Leeds and later in London, at Covent Garden, in 1958. She had previously sung this role and the role of Delilah in concert in 1950, in Sydney.

Der Schauspieldirektor
The Impresario

By Wolfgang Amadeus Mozart (1756-1791)   Text by Gottlieb Stephanie
First performed in Vienna, 1786

A one act comedy about two rival prima donnas and their theatrical impresario. The role of Madame Herz was first sung by Joan Sutherland at the 1957 Glyndebourne Festival.

Semiramide

By Gioacchino Rossini (1792-1868)   Text by Gaetano Rossi
First performed in Venice, 1823

Set in ancient Babylon, the opera tells of Semiramide, who has, with the help of her lover Assur, murdered her husband King Nino. Semiramide is now attracted to Arsace, a young army commander, who is in fact her unknown son. The relationship is eventually revealed, Semiramide dies saving Arsace from the jealous Assur and Arsace becomes the King of Babylon. Joan Sutherland first sang the role of Semiramide in 1962, at La Scala, Milan.

La Sonnambula
The Sleep-walker

By Vincenzo Bellini (1802-1835)   Text by Felice Romani
First performed in Milan, 1831

Set in a Swiss village in the early nineteenth century, the opera tells of Amina, who is loved by Elvino. He spurns her when she is found in the room of the visiting Count Rodolfo, at the local inn. It is later dramatically revealed that Amina is innocent and is in fact a sleep-walker. The opera ends with the reunion of Amina and Elvino. The title role of *La Sonnambula* entered Joan Sutherland's repertoire for the first time in 1960, in London.

LIST OF PERFORMANCES

DATE		PLACE	PERFORMANCE	COMPOSER	ROLE
26	November	London	*Carmen*	Bizet	Frasquita
2	December	London	*Aida*	Verdi	Priestess
7	December	London	*Aida*	Verdi	Priestess
11	December	London	*Aida*	Verdi	Priestess
12	December	London	*Carmen*	Bizet	Frasquita
18	December	London	*Aida*	Verdi	Priestess
26	December	London	*Aida*	Verdi	Priestess
28	December	London	*Carmen*	Bizet	Frasquita
31	December	London	*Carmen*	Bizet	Frasquita

—— 1954 ——

DATE		PLACE	PERFORMANCE	COMPOSER	ROLE
2	January	London	*Aida*	Verdi	Priestess
5	January	London	*Carmen*	Bizet	Frasquita
12	January	London	*Carmen*	Bizet	Frasquita
22	January	London	*Aida*	Verdi	Priestess
27	January	London	*Carmen*	Bizet	Frasquita
29	January	London	*Gloriana*	Britten	Lady Penelope Rich
2	February	London	*Gloriana*	Britten	Lady Penelope Rich
4	**February**	**London**	***Aida***	**Verdi**	**Aida**
9	February	London	*Carmen*	Bizet	Frasquita
12	February	London	*Carmen*	Bizet	Frasquita
16	February	London	*Gloriana*	Britten	Lady Penelope Rich
24	February	Croydon	*Aida*	Verdi	Priestess
26	February	Croydon	*Aida*	Verdi	Priestess
5	March	Croydon	*Die Walküre*	Wagner	Helmwige
8	March	Cardiff	*Carmen*	Bizet	Frasquita
9	March	Cardiff	*Die Walküre*	Wagner	Helmwige
11	March	Cardiff	*Gloriana*	Britten	Lady Penelope Rich
12	March	Cardiff	*Carmen*	Bizet	Frasquita
23	**March**	**Manchester**	***Der Freischütz***	**Weber**	**Agathe**
26	March	Manchester	*Der Freischütz*	Weber	Agathe
30	March	Manchester	*Gloriana*	Britten	Lady Penelope Rich
1	April	Manchester	*Carmen*	Bizet	Frasquita
2	April	Manchester	*Die Walküre*	Wagner	Helmwige
3	April	Manchester	*Aida*	Verdi	Priestess
5	April	Birmingham	*Carmen*	Bizet	Frasquita
6	April	Birmingham	*Die Walküre*	Wagner	Helmwige
13	April	Birmingham	*Gloriana*	Britten	Lady Penelope Rich
16	April	Birmingham	*Carmen*	Bizet	Frasquita
17	April	Birmingham	*Aida*	Verdi	Priestess
30	April	London	*Elektra*	R Strauss	Overseer
4	May	London	*Elektra*	R Strauss	Overseer
12	May	London	*Elektra*	R Strauss	Overseer
13	May	London	*Der Freischütz*	Weber	Agathe
27	**May**	**London**	***Das Rheingold***	**Wagner**	**Woglinde**
2	June	London	*Die Walküre*	Wagner	Helmwige
8	**June**	**London**	***Seigfried***	**Wagner**	**Woodbird**
17	June	London	*Götterdämmerung*	Wagner	Woglinde
21	June	London	*Das Rheingold*	Wagner	Woglinde
24	June	London	*Die Walküre*	Wagner	Helmwige
26	June	London	Concert		
26	June	London	*Seigfried*	Wagner	Woodbird
30	June	London	*Götterdämmerung*	Wagner	Woglinde
3	July	London	*Aida*	Verdi	Priestess
7	July	London	*Aida*	Verdi	Priestess
9	July	London	*Carmen*	Bizet	Frasquita
12	July	London	*Der Freischütz*	Weber	Agathe
16	July	London	*Der Freischütz*	Weber	Agathe
19	July	London	*Aida*	Verdi	Priestess
21	July	London	*Carmen*	Bizet	Frasquita
23	July	London	*Aida*	Verdi	Priestess
2	August	London	Promenade Concert		
28	October	London	*Carmen*	Bizet	Frasquita
30	October	London	*Carmen*	Bizet	Frasquita
17	**November**	**London**	***The Tales of Hoffmann***	**Offenbach**	**Antonia**
20	November	London	*The Tales of Hoffmann*	Offenbach	Antonia
23	November	London	*The Tales of Hoffmann*	Offenbach	Antonia
24	November	London	*Carmen*	Bizet	Frasquita
30	November	London	*Carmen*	Bizet	Frasquita
1	December	Landon	*The Tales of Hoffmann*	Offenbach	Antonia
4	December	London	*Carmen*	Bizet	Frasquita
7	December	London	*Carmen*	Bizet	Frasquita
13	December	London	*The Tales of Hoffmann*	Offenbach	Antonia
14	December	London	*Aida*	Verdi	Priestess
20	December	London	*Aida*	Verdi	Priestess

DATE		PLACE	PERFORMANCE	COMPOSER	ROLE
22	December	London	*Der Freischütz*	Weber	Agathe
28	December	London	*Aida*	Verdi	Priestess
30	December	London	*Der Freischütz*	Weber	Agathe

―――― 1955 ――――

DATE		PLACE	PERFORMANCE	COMPOSER	ROLE
15	January	London	*Der Freischütz*	Weber	Agathe
25	January	London	*Der Freischütz*	Weber	Agathe
27	**January**	**London**	***The Midsummer Marriage***	**Tippett**	**Jenifer**
31	January	London	*The Midsummer Marriage*	Tippett	Jenifer
8	February	London	*The Midsummer Marriage*	Tippett	Jenifer
11	February	London	*The Midsummer Marriage*	Tippett	Jenifer
22	February	London	*The Midsummer Marriage*	Tippett	Jenifer
28	**February**	**Glasgow**	***The Tales of Hoffmann***	**Offenbach**	**Giulietta**
1	March	Glasgow	*Aida*	Verdi	Aida
5	March	Glasgow	*The Tales of Hoffmann*	Offenbach	Giulietta, Antonia
7	March	Glasgow	*The Tales of Hoffmann*	Offenbach	Giulietta
14	March	Edinburgh	*The Tales of Hoffmann*	Offenbach	Giulietta
16	March	Edinburgh	*The Tales of Hoffmann*	Offenbach	Antonia
21	March	Leeds	*The Tales of Hoffmann*	Offenbach	Giulietta
28	March	Manchester	*The Tales of Hoffmann*	Offenbach	Giulietta
2	April	Manchester	*The Tales of Hoffmann*	Offenbach	Giulietta, Antonia
5	April	Manchester	*Aida*	Verdi	Aida
9	April	Manchester	*Aida*	Verdi	Aida
11	April	Coventry	*The Tales of Hoffmann*	Offenbach	Giulietta
13	April	Coventry	*The Tales of Hoffmann*	Offenbach	Antonia
23	April	London	*Aida*	Verdi	Aida
27	April	Brierly Hill, West Midlands	Concert		
10	May	London	*Das Rheingold*	Wagner	Woglinde
14	May	London	*Die Walküre*	Wagner	Helmwige
27	May	London	*Götterdämmerung*	Wagner	Woglinde
8	June	London	*Das Rheingold*	Wagner	Woglinde
10	June	London	*Die Walküre*	Wagner	Helmwige
16	**June**	**London**	***The Tales of Hoffmann***	**Offenbach**	**Olympia**
17	June	London	*Götterdämmerung*	Wagner	Woglinde
19	June	London	*The Tales of Hoffmann*	Offenbach	Olympia
22	June	London	*The Tales of Hoffmann*	Offenbach	Olympia
11	July	London	*Aida*	Verdi	Priestess
13	July	London	*Aida*	Verdi	Priestess
16	July	London	*Aida*	Verdi	Priestess
18	July	London	*Aida*	Verdi	Priestess
20	July	London	*The Tales of Hoffmann*	Offenbach	Olympia
22	July	London	*The Tales of Hoffmann*	Offenbach	Olympia
8	August	London	Concert *Te Deum*	Dvorak	
7	October	London	Recital		
12	October	Manchester	Concert		
20	**October**	**London**	***Carmen***	**Bizet**	**Micaela**
25	October	London	*Carmen*	Bizet	Micaela
30	October	Exeter	Concert *Aida*	Verdi	Aida
31	October	London	*Carmen*	Bizet	Micaela
4	November	London	*Carmen*	Bizet	Micaela
14	November	London	*Carmen*	Bizet	Micaela
19	November	London	*Carmen*	Bizet	Micaela
24	November	London	*Carmen*	Bizet	Micaela
30	November	London	*Carmen*	Bizet	Micaela
27	December	London	*Carmen*	Bizet	Micaela
29	December	London	*Carmen*	Bizet	Micaela

―――― 1956 ――――

DATE		PLACE	PERFORMANCE	COMPOSER	ROLE
24	March	Coventry	Concert *Requiem*	Verdi	
30	March	Cardiff	Concert *Messiah*	Handel	
19	April	London	*The Tales of Hoffmann*	Offenbach	Antonia
21	April	London	*The Tales of Hoffmann*	Offenbach	Antonia
24	April	London	*The Magic Flute*	Mozart	First Lady
27	April	London	*The Magic Flute*	Mozart	First Lady
2	May	London	Concert *Symphony No 4*	Mahler	
3	May	London	*The Magic Flute*	Mozart	First Lady
6	May	Brecon, Wales	Concert		
8	May	London	*The Magic Flute*	Mozart	First Lady
12	May	London	*The Magic Flute*	Mozart	First Lady
13	May	London	Concert *Magnificat*	Monteverdi	
24	May	London	*Das Rheingold*	Wagner	Woglinde
28	May	London	*Die Walküre*	Wagner	Helmwige
6	June	London	*Götterdämmerung*	Wagner	Woglinde
11	June	London	*Das Rheingold*	Wagner	Woglinde
12	June	London	*Die Walküre*	Wagner	Helmwige

DATE		PLACE	PERFORMANCE	COMPOSER	ROLE
16	June	London	*Götterdämmerung*	Wagner	Woglinde
18	June	London	*The Magic Flute*	Mozart	First Lady
20	June	London	*The Magic Flute*	Mozart	First Lady
28	June	London	*The Tales of Hoffmann*	Offenbach	Antonia
30	June	London	*The Magic Flute*	Mozart	First Lady
6	July	Glyndebourne	*Le Nozze di Figaro*	Mozart	Countess Almaviva
9	July	London	*The Tales of Hoffmann*	Offenbach	Antonia
10	July	Glyndebourne	*Le Nozze di Figaro*	Mozart	Countess Almaviva
14	July	Glyndebourne	*Le Nozze di Figaro*	Mozart	Countess Almaviva
18	July	Glyndebourne	*Le Nozze di Figaro*	Mozart	Countess Almaviva
19	July	Glyndebourne	*Die Zauberflöte*	Mozart	First Lady
20	July	Glyndebourne	*Le Nozze di Figaro*	Mozart	Countess Almaviva
22	July	Glyndebourne	*Die Zauberflöte*	Mozart	First Lady
25	July	Glyndebourne	*Die Zauberflöte*	Mozart	First Lady
27	July	Glyndebourne	*Le Nozze di Figaro*	Mozart	Countess Almaviva
3	August	Glyndebourne	*Die Zauberflöte*	Mozart	First Lady
7	August	Glyndebourne	*Die Zauberflöte*	Mozart	First Lady
9	August	Glyndebourne	*Die Zauberflöte*	Mozart	First Lady
11	August	Glyndebourne	*Die Zauberflöte*	Mozart	First Lady
13	August	Glyndebourne	*Die Zauberflöte*	Mozart	First Lady
3	September	London	Promenade Concert		
10	September	Liverpool	*Le Nozze di Figaro*	Mozart	Countess Almaviva
12	September	Liverpool	*Le Nozze di Figaro*	Mozart	Countess Almaviva
14	September	Liverpool	*Le Nozze di Figaro*	Mozart	Countess Almaviva
22	September	Liverpool	*Le Nozze di Figaro*	Mozart	Countess Almaviva
7	October	Llanelly, Wales	Concert		
27	October	Coventry	Concert *Mass in C Minor*	Mozart	
10	**November**	**London**	***The Magic Flute***	**Mozart**	**Pamina**
13	November	London	*The Magic Flute*	Mozart	Pamina
14	December	London	*The Magic Flute*	Mozart	Pamina
18	December	London	*The Magic Flute*	Mozart	Pamina
28	December	London	*The Magic Flute*	Mozart	Pamina

—— 1957 ——

DATE		PLACE	PERFORMANCE	COMPOSER	ROLE
28	**January**	**London**	***The Mastersingers of Nuremberg***	**Wagner**	**Eva**
31	January	London	*The Mastersingers of Nuremberg*	Wagner	Eva
5	February	London	*Carmen*	Bizet	Micaela
8	February	London	*The Mastersingers of Nuremberg*	Wagner	Eva
11	February	London	*The Mastersingers of Nuremberg*	Wagner	Eva
13	February	London	*The Mastersingers of Nuremberg*	Wagner	Eva
21	February	London	*The Midsummer Marriage*	Tippett	Jenifer
28	February	London	*The Midsummer Marriage*	Tippett	Jenifer
8	March	Cardiff	*The Magic Flute*	Mozart	Pamina
9	March	Cardiff	*The Magic Flute*	Mozart	Pamina
12	March	Cardiff	*The Magic Flute*	Mozart	Pamina
19	**March**	**London**	***Alcina***	**Handel**	**Alcina**
20	March	London	*Alcina*	Handel	Alcina
25	March	Manchester	*The Magic Flute*	Mozart	Pamina
29	March	Manchester	*The Magic Flute*	Mozart	Pamina
30	March	Manchester	*The Magic Flute*	Mozart	Pamina
8	April	Southampton	*The Magic Flute*	Mozart	Pamina
12	April	Southampton	*The Magic Flute*	Mozart	Pamina
13	April	Southampton	*The Magic Flute*	Mozart	Pamina
4	May	Swansea	Concert *Requiem*	Verdi	
8	**May**	**London**	***Rigoletto***	**Verdi**	**Gilda**
14	May	London	*Rigoletto*	Verdi	Gilda
17	May	London	*Rigoletto*	Verdi	Gilda
20	May	London	*Rigoletto*	Verdi	Gilda
28	May	London	*Rigoletto*	Verdi	Gilda
1	June	London	*Rigoletto*	Verdi	Gilda
25	June	London	*The Magic Flute*	Mozart	Pamina
28	June	London	*The Magic Flute*	Mozart	Pamina
5	**July**	**Glyndebourne**	***Der Schauspieldirektor***	**Mozart**	**Mme Herz**
7	July	Glyndebourne	*Der Schauspieldirektor*	Mozart	Mme Herz
12	July	Glyndebourne	*Der Schauspieldirektor*	Mozart	Mme Herz
14	July	Glyndebourne	*Der Schauspieldirektor*	Mozart	Mme Herz
15	July	London	*The Magic Flute*	Mozart	Pamina
16	July	Glyndebourne	*Der Schauspieldirektor*	Mozart	Mme Herz
17	July	London	*The Magic Flute*	Mozart	Pamina
18	July	Glyndebourne	*Der Schauspieldirektor*	Mozart	Mme Herz
20	July	Glyndebourne	*Der Schauspieldirektor*	Mozart	Mme Herz
23	July	Glyndebourne	*Der Schauspieldirektor*	Mozart	Mme Herz
11	September	London	Promenade Concert		
25	September	London	*Das Rheingold*	Wagner	Woglinde
4	October	London	*Götterdämmerung*	Wagner	Woglinde

DATE		PLACE	PERFORMANCE	COMPOSER	ROLE
7	October	London	*Das Rheingold*	Wagner	Woglinde
12	October	London	*Götterdämmerung*	Wagner	Woglinde
14	October	London	*Götterdämmerung*	Wagner	Woglinde
17	October	London	*Götterdämmerung*	Wagner	Woglinde
30	October	London	*The Tales of Hoffmann*	Offenbach	Antonia
31	October	London	*The Tales of Hoffmann*	Offenbach	Antonia
2	November	London	*Carmen*	Bizet	Micaela
5	November	London	*The Tales of Hoffmann*	Offenbach	Antonia
7	November	London	*The Tales of Hoffmann*	Offenbach	Antonia
8	November	London	*Carmen*	Bizet	Micaela
11	November	London	*Carmen*	Bizet	Micaela
13	November	London	*The Tales of Hoffmann*	Offenbach	Antonia
15	November	London	*Carmen*	Bizet	Micaela
18	November	London	*Carmen*	Bizet	Micaela
20	November	London	*Carmen*	Bizet	Micaela
21	November	London	*The Tales of Hoffmann*	Offenbach	Antonia
28	November	London	*Carmen*	Bizet	Micaela
2	December	London	*The Tales of Hoffmann*	Offenbach	Antonia
10	December	London	*Carmen*	Bizet	Micaela
18	December	London	*The Tales of Hoffmann*	Offenbach	Antonia
21	**December**	**London**	**Otello**	**Verdi**	**Desdemona**
27	December	London	*Otello*	Verdi	Desdemona
31	December	London	*Otello*	Verdi	Desdemona

——— 1958 ———

DATE		PLACE	PERFORMANCE	COMPOSER	ROLE
16	**January**	**London**	**The Dialogues of the Carmelites**	**Poulenc**	**Mme Lidoine**
18	January	London	*The Dialogues of the Carmelites*	Poulenc	Mme Lidoine
21	January	London	*The Dialogues of the Carmelites*	Poulenc	Mme Lidoine
24	January	London	*The Dialogues of the Carmelites*	Poulenc	Mme Lidoine
27	January	London	*The Dialogues of the Carmelites*	Poulenc	Mme Lidoine
5	February	London	*Rigoletto*	Verdi	Gilda
8	February	London	*Rigoletto*	Verdi	Gilda
10	February	London	*Rigoletto*	Verdi	Gilda
13	February	London	*Rigoletto*	Verdi	Gilda
18	February	London	*Rigoletto*	Verdi	Gilda
19	February	London	Concert		
21	February	London	*Rigoletto*	Verdi	Gilda
10	March	Oxford	*The Dialogues of the Carmelites*	Poulenc	Mme Lidoine
12	March	Oxford	*Rigoletto*	Verdi	Gilda
20	March	Manchester	*Carmen*	Bizet	Micaela
24	March	Manchester	*The Dialogues of the Carmelites*	Poulenc	Mme Lidoine
25	March	Manchester	*Rigoletto*	Verdi	Gilda
26	March	Manchester	*Rigoletto*	Verdi	Gilda
29	March	Manchester	*Rigoletto*	Verdi	Gilda
4	April	Liverpool	Concert *St Matthew Passion*	Bach	
5	April	London	*Rigoletto*	Verdi	Gilda
14	May	Manchester	Concert *Resurrection Symphony*	Mahler	
15	May	Manchester	Concert *Resurrection Symphony*	Mahler	
27	May	London	*Rigoletto*	Verdi	Gilda
9	June	London	Royal Opera House Centenary Gala		
24	June	London	*Carmen*	Bizet	Micaela
7	July	London	*Carmen*	Bizet	Micaela
26	**July**	**Vancouver**	**Don Giovanni**	**Mozart**	**Donna Anna**
29	July	Vancouver	*Don Giovanni*	Mozart	Donna Anna
31	July	Vancouver	*Don Giovanni*	Mozart	Donna Anna
5	August	Vancouver	*Don Giovanni*	Mozart	Donna Anna
7	August	Vancouver	*Don Giovanni*	Mozart	Donna Anna
9	August	Vancouver	*Don Giovanni*	Mozart	Donna Anna
19	September	London	*Das Rheingold*	Wagner	Woglinde
29	September	London	*Siegfried*	Wagner	Woodbird
3	October	London	*Götterdämmerung*	Wagner	Woglinde
4	October	Sevenoaks, Kent	Recital		
6	October	London	*Das Rheingold*	Wagner	Woglinde
9	October	London	*Siegfried*	Wagner	Woodbird
11	October	London	*Götterdämmerung*	Wagner	Woglinde
14	**October**	**Leeds**	**Samson**	**Handel**	**Israelite woman**
15	October	Leeds	*Samson*	Handel	Israelite woman
16	October	Leeds	*Samson*	Handel	Israelite woman
17	October	Leeds	*Samson*	Handel	Israelite woman
18	October	Leeds	*Samson*	Handel	Israelite woman
25	October	Horsham, Sussex	Recital		
15	November	London	*Samson*	Handel	Israelite woman
18	November	London	*Samson*	Handel	Israelite woman
19	November	Leeds	Concert		
24	November	Dublin	*Don Giovanni*	Mozart	Donna Anna

DATE		PLACE	PERFORMANCE	COMPOSER	ROLE
26	November	Dublin	*Don Giovanni*	Mozart	Donna Anna
28	November	Dublin	*Don Giovanni*	Mozart	Donna Anna
29	November	Dublin	Concert		
1	December	Dublin	*Don Giovanni*	Mozart	Donna Anna
11	December	London	*Samson*	Handel	Israelite woman
20	December	Liverpool	Concert *Messiah*	Handel	
27	December	Liverpool	Concert *Messiah*	Handel	

—— 1959 ——

2	January	Liverpool	Concert *Messiah*	Handel	
3	January	London	*Samson*	Handel	Israelite woman
17	**February**	**London**	***Lucia di Lammermoor***	**Donizetti**	**Lucia**
20	February	London	*Lucia di Lammermoor*	Donizetti	Lucia
23	February	London	*Lucia di Lammermoor*	Donizetti	Lucia
26	February	London	*Lucia di Lammermoor*	Donizetti	Lucia
28	February	London	*Lucia di Lammermoor*	Donizetti	Lucia
6	May	Manchester	Concert *Symphony No 9*	Beethoven	
7	May	Manchester	Concert *Symphony No 9*	Beethoven	
8	June	London	*Samson*	Handel	Israelite woman
12	June	London	*Samson*	Handel	Israelite woman
18	June	London	Recital		
24	**June**	**London**	***Rodelinda***	**Handel**	**Rodelinda**
25	June	London	*Samson*	Handel	Israelite woman
26	June	London	*Rodelinda*	Handel	Rodelinda
10	July	London	*Lucia di Lammermoor*	Donizetti	Lucia
14	July	London	*Lucia di Lammermoor*	Donizetti	Lucia
16	July	London	*Lucia di Lammermoor*	Donizetti	Lucia
18	July	London	*Lucia di Lammermoor*	Donizetti	Lucia
18	October	London	Concert *Don Giovanni*	Mozart	Donna Anna
20	October	London	Concert *Don Giovanni*	Mozart	Donna Anna
27	October	London	Concert		
31	October	London	Concert		
3	November	Manchester	Recital		
8	November	London	Concert		
28	November	London	Concert *Symphony No 9*	Beethoven	
30	November	London	Concert *Symphony No 9*	Beethoven	
3	December	Vienna	*Don Giovanni*	Mozart	Donna Anna
5	December	Vienna	*Don Giovanni*	Mozart	Donna Anna
17	December	Vienna	*Otello*	Verdi	Desdemona
19	December	Vienna	*Otello*	Verdi	Desdemona
30	December	Liverpool	Concert *Messiah*	Handel	

—— 1960 ——

2	January	Liverpool	Concert *Messiah*	Handel	
8	**January**	**London**	***La Traviata***	**Verdi**	**Violetta**
22	January	London	*La Traviata*	Verdi	Violetta
27	January	London	*La Traviata*	Verdi	Violetta
28	January	Birmingham	Concert *Symphony No 4*	Mahler	
30	January	London	*La Traviata*	Verdi	Violetta
5	February	London	*Lucia di Lammermoor*	Donizetti	Lucia
8	February	London	*Lucia di Lammermoor*	Donizetti	Lucia
10	February	London	*Lucia di Lammermoor*	Donizetti	Lucia
13	February	London	*Lucia di Lammermoor*	Donizetti	Lucia
19	February	Venice	*Alcina*	Handel	Alcina
21	February	Venice	*Alcina*	Handel	Alcina
23	February	Venice	*Alcina*	Handel	Alcina
11	March	Palermo	*Lucia di Lammermoor*	Donizetti	Lucia
13	March	Palermo	*Lucia di Lammermoor*	Donizetti	Lucia
15	March	Palermo	*Lucia di Lammermoor*	Donizetti	Lucia
20	March	Palermo	*Lucia di Lammermoor*	Donizetti	Lucia
31	March	Genoa	*Lucia di Lammermoor*	Donizetti	Lucia
3	April	Genoa	*Lucia di Lammermoor*	Donizetti	Lucia
5	April	Genoa	*Lucia di Lammermoor*	Donizetti	Lucia
25	April	Paris	*Lucia di Lammermoor*	Donizetti	Lucia
30	April	Paris	*Lucia di Lammermoor*	Donizetti	Lucia
4	May	London	*La Traviata*	Verdi	Violetta
7	May	Paris	*Lucia di Lammermoor*	Donizetti	Lucia
14	May	London	*La Traviata*	Verdi	Violetta
24	**May**	**Glyndebourne**	***I Puritani***	**Bellini**	**Elvira**
26	May	Glyndebourne	*I Puritani*	Bellini	Elvira
28	May	Glyndebourne	*I Puritani*	Bellini	Elvira
1	June	Glyndebourne	*I Puritani*	Bellini	Elvira
3	June	Glyndebourne	*I Puritani*	Bellini	Elvira
5	June	Glyndebourne	*I Puritani*	Bellini	Elvira

DATE		PLACE	PERFORMANCE	COMPOSER	ROLE
9	June	Glyndebourne	*I Puritani*	Bellini	Elvira
12	June	London	Concert *Requiem*	Verdi	
14	June	Glyndebourne	*I Puritani*	Bellini	Elvira
18	June	Glyndebourne	*I Puritani*	Bellini	Elvira
19	June	London	Concert *Samson*	Handel	Israelite woman
24	June	Glyndebourne	*I Puritani*	Bellini	Elvira
1	July	Glyndebourne	*Don Giovanni*	Mozart	Donna Anna
3	July	Glyndebourne	*Don Giovanni*	Mozart	Donna Anna
5	July	Glyndebourne	*Don Giovanni*	Mozart	Donna Anna
7	July	Glyndebourne	*Don Giovanni*	Mozart	Donna Anna
9	July	Glyndebourne	*Don Giovanni*	Mozart	Donna Anna
11	July	Glyndebourne	*Don Giovanni*	Mozart	Donna Anna
16	July	Glyndebourne	*Don Giovanni*	Mozart	Donna Anna
20	July	Glyndebourne	*Don Giovanni*	Mozart	Donna Anna
22	July	Glyndebourne	*Don Giovanni*	Mozart	Donna Anna
24	July	Glyndebourne	*Don Giovanni*	Mozart	Donna Anna
29	July	Glyndebourne	*Don Giovanni*	Mozart	Donna Anna
1	August	London	Promenade Concert		
3	August	Glyndebourne	*Don Giovanni*	Mozart	Donna Anna
5	August	Glyndebourne	*Don Giovanni*	Mozart	Donna Anna
7	August	Worthing	Recital		
13	August	London	Promenade Concert		
21	August	Edinburgh	Concert *Requiem*	Verdi	
24	August	Edinburgh	*I Puritani*	Bellini	Elvira
26	August	Edinburgh	*I Puritani*	Bellini	Elvira
31	August	Edinburgh	*I Puritani*	Bellini	Elvira
3	September	Edinburgh	*I Puritani*	Bellini	Elvira
8	September	Edinburgh	*I Puritani*	Bellini	Elvira
10	September	Edinburgh	*I Puritani*	Bellini	Elvira
4	October	Liverpool	Concert		
19	**October**	**London**	***La Sonnambula***	**Bellini**	**Amina**
21	October	London	*La Sonnambula*	Bellini	Amina
25	October	London	*La Sonnambula*	Bellini	Amina
27	October	London	Recital		
28	October	London	*La Sonnambula*	Bellini	Amina
31	October	London	*La Sonnambula*	Bellini	Amina
3	November	London	*La Sonnambula*	Bellini	Amina
7	November	London	*La Sonnambula*	Bellini	Amina
16	November	Dallas	*Alcina*	Handel	Alcina
18	November	Dallas	*Alcina*	Handel	Alcina
20	November	Dallas	*Don Giovanni*	Mozart	Donna Anna
23	November	Dallas	*Don Giovanni*	Mozart	Donna Anna
29	November	Keele, Staffordshire	Recital		
1	December	London	*La Sonnambula*	Bellini	Amina
3	December	London	*La Sonnambula*	Bellini	Amina
5	December	London	*La Sonnambula*	Bellini	Amina
9	December	London	*Lucia di Lammermoor*	Donizetti	Lucia
11	December	London	Concert		
13	December	London	*Lucia di Lammermoor*	Donizetti	Lucia
16	December	London	*Lucia di Lammermoor*	Donizetti	Lucia
22	December	London	*Lucia di Lammermoor*	Donizetti	Lucia
30	December	Barcelona	*I Puritani*	Bellini	Elvira

	1961				
3	January	Barcelona	*I Puritani*	Bellini	Elvira
6	January	Barcelona	*I Puritani*	Bellini	Elvira
12	January	Palermo	*I Puritani*	Bellini	Elvira
15	January	Palermo	*I Puritani*	Bellini	Elvira
17	January	Palermo	*I Puritani*	Bellini	Elvira
24	January	Venice	*Lucia di Lammermoor*	Donizetti	Lucia
26	January	Venice	*Lucia di Lammermoor*	Donizetti	Lucia
29	January	Venice	*Lucia di Lammermoor*	Donizetti	Lucia
2	February	Rock Hill, South Carolina	Recital		
5	February	Danbury, Connecticut	Recital		
7	February	Washington, DC	Concert		
11	February	Mt Lebanon, Pittsburgh	Recital		
13	February	Oklahoma	Recital		
15	February	Dallas	Concert		
21	February	New York	Concert *Beatrice di Tenda*	Bellini	Beatrice
23	February	Englewood, New Jersey	Recital		
25	February	Richmond	Recital		
27	February	Vancouver	Recital		
1	March	New York	Concert *Beatrice di Tenda*	Bellini	Beatrice
6	March	Aurora, New York	Recital		
9	March	Montreal	Recital		

DATE		PLACE	PERFORMANCE	COMPOSER	ROLE
11	March	New York	Concert *Beatrice di Tenda*	Bellini	Beatrice
13	March	Toronto	Recital		
22	March	Genoa	*I Puritani*	Bellini	Elvira
26	March	Genoa	*I Puritani*	Bellini	Elvira
29	March	Genoa	*I Puritani*	Bellini	Elvira
14	April	Milan	*Lucia di Lammermoor*	Donizetti	Lucia
17	April	Milan	*Lucia di Lammermoor*	Donizetti	Lucia
20	April	Milan	*Lucia di Lammermoor*	Donizetti	Lucia
27	April	Milan	*Lucia di Lammermoor*	Donizetti	Lucia
3	May	Milan	*Lucia di Lammermoor*	Donizetti	Lucia
10	**May**	**Milan**	***Beatrice di Tenda***	**Bellini**	**Beatrice**
13	May	Milan	*Beatrice di Tenda*	Bellini	Beatrice
17	May	Milan	*Beatrice di Tenda*	Bellini	Beatrice
19	May	Milan	*Beatrice di Tenda*	Bellini	Beatrice
21	May	Milan	*Beatrice di Tenda*	Bellini	Beatrice
6	June	London	*Lucia di Lammermoor*	Donizetti	Lucia
9	June	London	*Lucia di Lammermoor*	Donizetti	Lucia
12	June	London	*Lucia di Lammermoor*	Donizetti	Lucia
16	June	Paris	*Lucia di Lammermoor*	Donizetti	Lucia
19	June	Paris	*Lucia di Lammermoor*	Donizetti	Lucia
24	June	Paris	*Lucia di Lammermoor*	Donizetti	Lucia
25	August	Edinburgh	*Lucia di Lammermoor*	Donizetti	Lucia
28	August	Edinburgh	*Lucia di Lammermoor*	Donizetti	Lucia
1	September	Edinburgh	*Lucia di Lammermoor*	Donizetti	Lucia
4	September	Edinburgh	Concert		
23	September	San Francisco	*Lucia di Lammermoor*	Donizetti	Lucia
25	September	Lawrence, Kansas	Recital		
28	September	Omaha, Nebraska	Recital		
30	September	Atlanta	Recital		
2	October	Syracuse, New York	Recital		
4	October	Hartford, Connecticut	Recital		
9	October	New York	Concert		
14	October	Chicago	*Lucia di Lammermoor*	Donizetti	Lucia
16	October	Chicago	*Lucia di Lammermoor*	Donizetti	Lucia
18	October	Chicago	*Lucia di Lammermoor*	Donizetti	Lucia
20	October	Montclair, New Jersey	Recital		
23	October	Worcester, Massachucetts	Concert		
25	October	San Francisco	*Lucia di Lammermoor*	Donizetti	Lucia
29	October	Los Angeles	*Lucia di Lammermoor*	Donizetti	Lucia
2	November	San Diego	*Lucia di Lammermoor*	Donizetti	Lucia
4	November	Los Angeles	*Lucia di Lammermoor*	Donizetti	Lucia
7	November	San Francisco	Recital		
11	November	Dallas	Recital		
16	November	Dallas	*Lucia di Lammermoor*	Donizetti	Lucia
18	November	Dallas	*Lucia di Lammermoor*	Donizetti	Lucia
20	November	New Brunswick, New Jersey	Recital		
26	November	New York	*Lucia di Lammermoor*	Donizetti	Lucia
28	November	Princeton, New Jersey	Recital		
2	December	New York	*Lucia di Lammermoor*	Donizetti	Lucia
5	December	New York	Concert *La Sonnambula*	Bellini	Amina
9	December	New York	*Lucia di Lammermoor*	Donizetti	Lucia
11	December	Washington, DC	Recital		
13	December	Great Neck, New York	Recital		
15	December	New York	*Lucia di Lammermoor*	Donizetti	Lucia
17	December	Philadelphia	Concert *La Sonnambula*	Bellini	Amina
21	December	New York	*Lucia di Lammermoor*	Donizetti	Lucia

—— 1962 ——					
4	**January**	**London**	***Die Zauberflöte***	**Mozart**	**Queen of the Night**
6	January	London	*Die Zauberflöte*	Mozart	Queen of the Night
8	January	London	*Die Zauberflöte*	Mozart	Queen of the Night
21	January	Palermo	*Lucia di Lammermoor*	Donizetti	Lucia
25	January	Rome	Concert		
28	January	Barcelona	*Lucia di Lammermoor*	Donizetti	Lucia
1	February	Barcelona	*Lucia di Lammermoor*	Donizetti	Lucia
10	February	Milan	*La Sonnambula*	Bellini	Amina
13	February	Milan	*La Sonnambula*	Bellini	Amina
15	February	Milan	*La Sonnambula*	Bellini	Amina
18	February	Milan	*La Sonnambula*	Bellini	Amina
20	February	Milan	*La Sonnambula*	Bellini	Amina
23	February	Antwerp	Concert		
25	February	Amsterdam	Concert		
8	March	London	*Alcina*	Handel	Alcina
10	March	London	*Alcina*	Handel	Alcina
14	March	London	*Alcina*	Handel	Alcina

DATE		PLACE	PERFORMANCE	COMPOSER	ROLE
17	March	London	*Alcina*	Handel	Alcina
21	March	London	*La Traviata*	Verdi	Violetta
24	March	London	*La Traviata*	Verdi	Violetta
26	March	London	*La Traviata*	Verdi	Violetta
29	March	London	*La Traviata*	Verdi	Violetta
1	April	London	Concert		
4	April	London	*La Traviata*	Verdi	Violetta
7	April	London	*La Traviata*	Verdi	Violetta
12	April	Milan	*La Sonnambula*	Bellini	Amina
15	April	Milan	*La Sonnambula*	Bellini	Amina
18	April	Milan	*La Sonnambula*	Bellini	Amina
23	April	Milan	*La Sonnambula*	Bellini	Amina
4	May	Naples	*Beatrice di Tenda*	Bellini	Beatrice
6	May	Naples	*Beatrice di Tenda*	Bellini	Beatrice
28	**May**	**Milan**	***Gli Ugonotti***	**Meyerbeer**	**Margherita di Valois**
31	May	Milan	*Gli Ugonotti*	Meyerbeer	Margherita di Valois
2	June	Milan	*Gli Ugonotti*	Meyerbeer	Margherita di Valois
7	June	Milan	*Gli Ugonotti*	Meyerbeer	Margherita di Valois
12	June	Milan	*Gli Ugonotti*	Meyerbeer	Margherita di Valois
24	July	New York	Concert		
26	July	Chicago	Concert		
2	August	Hollywood	Concert		
5	October	Rosehill, Cumberland	Recital		
7	October	Rosehill, Cumberland	Recital		
17	**December**	**Milan**	***Semiramide***	**Rossini**	**Semiramide**
19	December	Milan	*Semiramide*	Rossini	Semiramide
22	December	Milan	*Semiramide*	Rossini	Semiramide
26	December	Milan	*Semiramide*	Rossini	Semiramide
29	December	Milan	*Semiramide*	Rossini	Semiramide

—— 1963 ——

1	January	Milan	*Semiramide*	Rossini	Semiramide
5	January	Milan	*Semiramide*	Rossini	Semiramide
17	January	Washington, DC	Kennedy Inaugural Anniversary Concert		
25	January	Philadelphia	Concert		
6	February	White Plains, New York	Concert		
21	February	New York	*La Sonnambula*	Bellini	Amina
23	February	Boston	Concert		
27	February	New York	*La Sonnambula*	Bellini	Amina
4	March	New York	*La Sonnambula*	Bellini	Amina
7	March	New York	*La Sonnambula*	Bellini	Amina
9	March	Englewood, New Jersey	Concert		
10	March	Newark	Concert		
14	March	New York	*La Sonnambula*	Bellini	Amina
16	March	New York	Concert		
19	March	New York	*La Sonnambula*	Bellini	Amina
23	March	New York	*La Sonnambula*	Bellini	Amina
26	March	New York	Concert		
30	March	New York	*La Sonnambula*	Bellini	Amina
2	April	New York	*La Sonnambula*	Bellini	Amina
5	April	Los Angeles	Concert		
7	April	San Francisco	Concert		
12	April	New York	*La Sonnambula*	Bellini	Amina
16	April	New York	Concert *I Puritani*	Bellini	Elvira
18	April	Philadelphia	Concert *I Puritani*	Bellini	Elvira
24	April	New York	Concert *I Puritani*	Bellini	Elvira
27	April	Washington, DC	Concert		
10	June	Croydon, Surrey	Concert		
20	**June**	**London**	***Giulio Cesare***	**Handel**	**Cleopatra**
22	June	London	*Giulio Cesare*	Handel	Cleopatra
26	June	London	*Giulio Cesare*	Handel	Cleopatra
14	September	San Francisco	*La Sonnambula*	Bellini	Amina
17	September	San Francisco	*La Sonnambula*	Bellini	Amina
22	September	San Francisco	*La Sonnambula*	Bellini	Amina
17	**October**	**Vancouver**	***Norma***	**Bellini**	**Norma**
19	October	Vancouver	*Norma*	Bellini	Norma
22	October	Vancouver	*Norma*	Bellini	Norma
24	October	Vancouver	*Norma*	Bellini	Norma
26	October	Vancouver	*Norma*	Bellini	Norma
29	October	Vancouver	Concert		
2	November	Los Angeles	*La Sonnambula*	Bellini	Amina
4	November	Los Angeles	*La Sonnambula*	Bellini	Amina
12	November	Philadelphia	*La Traviata*	Verdi	Violetta
22	November	Toronto	Concert		
5	December	New York	*La Sonnambula*	Bellini	Amina

DATE		PLACE	PERFORMANCE		COMPOSER	ROLE
10	December	New York	*La Sonnambula*		Bellini	Amina
14	December	New York	*La Traviata*		Verdi	Violetta
23	December	New York	*La Sonnambula*		Bellini	Amina
28	December	New York	*La Traviata*		Verdi	Violetta
——— 1964 ———						
2	January	New York	*La Traviata*		Verdi	Violetta
5	January	New York	Metropolitan Opera Gala			
8	January	New York	*La Sonnambula*		Bellini	Amina
11	January	New York	*La Traviata*		Verdi	Violetta
14	January	Cleveland, Ohio	Concert			
17	January	New York	*La Traviata*		Verdi	Violetta
21	January	New York	*La Traviata*		Verdi	Violetta
24	January	New York	*La Traviata*		Verdi	Violetta
29	January	Los Angeles	Concert	*Semiramide*	Rossini	Semiramide
31	January	Los Angeles	Concert	*Semiramide*	Rossini	Semiramide
14	February	Boston	*I Puritani*		Bellini	Elvira
18	February	New York	Concert	*Semiramide*	Rossini	Semiramide
20	February	New York	Concert	*Semiramide*	Rossini	Semiramide
22	February	Hartford, Connecticut	Concert			
20	March	London	*I Puritani*		Bellini	Elvira
23	March	London	*I Puritani*		Bellini	Elvira
26	March	London	*I Puritani*		Bellini	Elvira
30	March	London	*I Puritani*		Bellini	Elvira
1	April	London	*I Puritani*		Bellini	Elvira
4	April	London	*I Puritani*		Bellini	Elvira
7	April	London	*I Puritani*		Bellini	Elvira
10	April	London	*I Puritani*		Bellini	Elvira
19	April	Boston	*Lucia di Lammermoor*		Donizetti	Lucia
23	April	Cleveland, Ohio	*Lucia di Lammermoor*		Donizetti	Lucia
30	April	Michigan	Concert			
3	May	New York	*La Sonnambula*		Bellini	Amina
9	May	New York	*La Sonnambula*		Bellini	Amina
16	May	Atlanta, Georgia	*Lucia di Lammermoor*		Donizetti	Lucia
23	May	Minneapolis	*Lucia di Lammermoor*		Donizetti	Lucia
26	May	Detroit	*Lucia di Lammermoor*		Donizetti	Lucia
4	June	Berne	Concert			
12	June	Milan	*Lucia di Lammermoor*		Donizetti	Lucia
15	June	Milan	*Lucia di Lammermoor*		Donizetti	Lucia
18	June	Milan	*Lucia di Lammermoor*		Donizetti	Lucia
20	June	Milan	*Lucia di Lammermoor*		Donizetti	Lucia
23	June	Milan	*Lucia di Lammermoor*		Donizetti	Lucia
12	October	New York	*Lucia di Lammermoor*		Donizetti	Lucia
16	October	New York	*Lucia di Lammermoor*		Donizetti	Lucia
24	October	New York	*Lucia di Lammermoor*		Donizetti	Lucia
27	October	New York	*Lucia di Lammermoor*		Donizetti	Lucia
1	November	San Fransciso	*La Traviata*		Verdi	Violetta
3	November	San Fransciso	*La Traviata*		Verdi	Violetta
5	November	San Fransciso	*La Traviata*		Verdi	Violetta
8	November	Los Angeles	*La Traviata*		Verdi	Violetta
10	November	Los Angeles	*La Traviata*		Verdi	Violetta
14	November	New York	*Lucia di Lammermoor*		Donizetti	Lucia
24	November	New York	*Lucia di Lammermoor*		Donizetti	Lucia
29	November	New York	Metropolitan Opera Gala			
8	December	Montreal	Concert			
17	December	Houston	Concert			
19	December	Houston	Concert			
——— 1965 ———						
3	January	New York	Concert	*Alcina*	Handel	Alcina
5	January	New York	Concert	*Alcina*	Handel	Alcina
9	January	Cincinnatti, Ohio	Concert			
17	January	New Orleans	Concert			
5	February	Boston	*Semiramide*		Rossini	Semiramide
7	February	Boston	*Semiramide*		Rossini	Semiramide
15	February	Miami	*Lucia di Lammermoor*		Donizetti	Lucia
17	February	Miami Beach	*Lucia di Lammermoor*		Donizetti	Lucia
20	February	Miami	*Lucia di Lammermoor*		Donizetti	Lucia
23	February	Fort Lauderdale, Florida	*Lucia di Lammermoor*		Donizetti	Lucia
9	**March**	**Philadelphia**	***Faust***		**Gounod**	**Marguerite**
16	March	Hartford, Connecticut	*Faust*		Gounod	Marguerite
21	March	Bloomington, Indiana	Concert			
3	May	London	*Lucia di Lammermoor*		Donizetti	Lucia
6	May	London	*Lucia di Lammermoor*		Donizetti	Lucia

DATE		PLACE	PERFORMANCE	COMPOSER	ROLE
8	May	London	*Lucia di Lammermoor*	Donizetti	Lucia
11	May	London	*Lucia di Lammermoor*	Donizetti	Lucia
17	May	London	*Lucia di Lammermoor*	Donizetti	Lucia
26	May	London	*La Sonnambula*	Bellini	Amina
29	May	London	*La Sonnambula*	Bellini	Amina
1	June	London	*La Sonnambula*	Bellini	Amina
4	June	London	*La Sonnambula*	Bellini	Amina
7	June	London	*La Sonnambula*	Bellini	Amina
10	June	London	*La Sonnambula*	Bellini	Amina
10	July	Melbourne	*Lucia di Lammermoor*	Donizetti	Lucia
12	July	Melbourne	*Lucia di Lammermoor*	Donizetti	Lucia
14	July	Melbourne	*Lucia di Lammermoor*	Donizetti	Lucia
17	July	Melbourne	*Lucia di Lammermoor*	Donizetti	Lucia
20	July	Melbourne	*La Traviata*	Verdi	Violetta
22	July	Melbourne	*La Traviata*	Verdi	Violetta
24	July	Melbourne	*La Traviata*	Verdi	Violetta
26	July	Melbourne	*La Traviata*	Verdi	Violetta
29	July	Melbourne	*Semiramide*	Rossini	Semiramide
31	July	Melbourne	*Semiramide*	Rossini	Semiramide
3	August	Melbourne	*La Sonnambula*	Bellini	Amina
5	August	Melbourne	*La Sonnambula*	Bellini	Amina
7	August	Melbourne	*Semiramide*	Rossini	Semiramide
10	August	Melbourne	*Faust*	Gounod	Marguerite
12	August	Melbourne	*Faust*	Gounod	Marguerite
14	August	Melbourne	*La Sonnambula*	Bellini	Amina
16	August	Adelaide	*Lucia di Lammermoor*	Donizetti	Lucia
18	August	Adelaide	*Lucia di Lammermoor*	Donizetti	Lucia
21	August	Adelaide	*Faust*	Gounod	Marguerite
23	August	Adelaide	*Faust*	Gounod	Marguerite
25	August	Adelaide	*La Traviata*	Verdi	Violetta
27	August	Adelaide	*La Traviata*	Verdi	Violetta
31	August	Sydney	*Lucia di Lammermoor*	Donizetti	Lucia
2	September	Sydney	*Lucia di Lammermoor*	Donizetti	Lucia
4	September	Sydney	*Semiramide*	Rossini	Semiramide
6	September	Sydney	*Semiramide*	Rossini	Semiramide
9	September	Sydney	*Faust*	Gounod	Marguerite
11	September	Sydney	*La Sonnambula*	Bellini	Amina
13	September	Sydney	*Faust*	Gounod	Marguerite
16	September	Sydney	*La Traviata*	Verdi	Violetta
18	September	Sydney	*La Traviata*	Verdi	Violetta
20	September	Sydney	*La Traviata*	Verdi	Violetta
22	September	Sydney	*Semiramide*	Rossini	Semiramide
24	September	Sydney	*La Sonnambula*	Bellini	Amina
27	September	Sydney	*La Traviata*	Verdi	Violetta
29	September	Sydney	*Semiramide*	Rossini	Semiramide
2	October	Sydney	*Lucia di Lammermoor*	Donizetti	Lucia
4	October	Sydney	*Semiramide*	Rossini	Semiramide
6	October	Sydney	*La Traviata*	Verdi	Violetta
9	October	Sydney	*La Sonnambula*	Bellini	Amina
11	October	Brisbane	*Lucia di Lammermoor*	Donizetti	Lucia
13	October	Brisbane	*La Traviata*	Verdi	Violetta
16	October	Brisbane	*Lucia di Lammermoor*	Donizetti	Lucia
	1966				
20	February	London	Concert		
25	February	Copenhagen	*Lucia di Lammermoor*	Donizetti	Lucia
28	February	Copenhagen	*Lucia di Lammermoor*	Donizetti	Lucia
3	March	Copenhagen	*Lucia di Lammermoor*	Donizetti	Lucia
18	March	Antwerp	Concert		
19	April	Milan	*Don Giovanni*	Mozart	Donna Anna
21	April	Milan	*Don Giovanni*	Mozart	Donna Anna
25	April	Milan	*Don Giovanni*	Mozart	Donna Anna
28	April	Paris	Concert		
30	April	Milan	*Don Giovanni*	Mozart	Donna Anna
3	May	Stuttgart	Concert		
6	May	Stuttgart	Concert		
2	**June**	**London**	***La Fille du Régiment***	**Donizetti**	**Marie**
8	June	London	*La Fille du Régiment*	Donizetti	Marie
11	June	London	*La Fille du Régiment*	Donizetti	Marie
14	June	London	*La Fille du Régiment*	Donizetti	Marie
17	June	London	*La Fille du Régiment*	Donizetti	Marie
23	June	London	*La Fille du Régiment*	Donizetti	Marie
27	June	London	*La Fille du Régiment*	Donizetti	Marie
30	June	Oxford	Concert		
2	July	London	*La Fille du Régiment*	Donizetti	Marie

DATE		PLACE	PERFORMANCE	COMPOSER	ROLE
20	September	San Francisco	*I Puritani*	Bellini	Elvira
23	September	San Francisco	*I Puritani*	Bellini	Elvira
29	September	San Francisco	*I Puritani*	Bellini	Elvira
2	October	San Francisco	*I Puritani*	Bellini	Elvira
5	October	Sacramento	*I Puritani*	Bellini	Elvira
8	October	San Francisco	*I Puritani*	Bellini	Elvira
15	October	San Antonio, Texas	Concert		
20	October	Atlanta, Georgia	Concert		
26	October	White Plains, New York	Concert		
1	November	Philadelphia	*Lucia di Lammermoor*	Donizetti	Lucia
4	November	Philadelphia	*Lucia di Lammermoor*	Donizetti	Lucia
19	November	Los Angeles	Concert		
21	November	Los Angeles	Concert		
26	November	Los Angeles	Concert		
30	November	Houston	Concert		
12	December	New York	*Lucia di Lammermoor*	Donizetti	Lucia
17	December	Washington, DC	Concert		
21	December	New York	*Lucia di Lammermoor*	Donizetti	Lucia
24	December	New York	*Lucia di Lammermoor*	Donizetti	Lucia
28	December	New York	*Lucia di Lammermoor*	Donizetti	Lucia
31	December	New York	*Lucia di Lammermoor*	Donizetti	Lucia

—— 1967 ——

4	January	New York	*Don Giovanni*	Mozart	Donna Anna
9	January	New York	*Don Giovanni*	Mozart	Donna Anna
12	January	New York	*Don Giovanni*	Mozart	Donna Anna
17	January	New York	*Don Giovanni*	Mozart	Donna Anna
21	January	Philadelphia	Concert		
28	January	New York	*Don Giovanni*	Mozart	Donna Anna
2	February	Toronto	Concert		
6	February	Boston	*Don Giovanni*	Mozart	Donna Anna
8	February	Boston	*Don Giovanni*	Mozart	Donna Anna
11	February	Newark, New Jersey	Concert		
15	February	Boston	*Don Giovanni*	Mozart	Donna Anna
23	February	Bloomington, Indiana	Concert		
28	February	Montreal	Concert		
11	March	Vancouver	*Lucia di Lammermoor*	Donizetti	Lucia
15	March	Vancouver	*Lucia di Lammermoor*	Donizetti	Lucia
22	March	Vancouver	*Lucia di Lammermoor*	Donizetti	Lucia
25	March	Vancouver	*Lucia di Lammermoor*	Donizetti	Lucia
29	March	Vancouver	*Lucia di Lammermoor*	Donizetti	Lucia
10	**April**	**Seattle**	***Lakmé***	**Delibes**	**Lakmé**
13	April	Seattle	*Lakmé*	Delibes	Lakmé
15	April	Seattle	*Lakmé*	Delibes	Lakmé
19	April	Seattle	*Lakmé*	Delibes	Lakmé
22	April	Seattle	*Lakmé*	Delibes	Lakmé
21	**May**	**Vienna**	***Orfeo ed Euridice***	**Haydn**	**Euridice**
25	May	Vienna	*Orfeo ed Euridice*	Haydn	Euridice
29	May	Vienna	*Orfeo ed Euridice*	Haydn	Euridice
2	June	Vienna	*Orfeo ed Euridice*	Haydn	Euridice
6	June	Vienna	*Orfeo ed Euridice*	Haydn	Euridice
24	June	London	*La Fille du Régiment*	Donizetti	Marie
27	June	London	*La Fille du Régiment*	Donizetti	Marie
4	July	London	Royal Opera House Gala		
7	July	London	*La Fille du Régiment*	Donizetti	Marie
11	July	London	*La Fille du Régiment*	Donizetti	Marie
15	July	London	*La Fille du Régiment*	Donizetti	Marie
25	August	Edinburgh	*Orfeo ed Euridice*	Haydn	Euridice
29	August	Edinburgh	*Orfeo ed Euridice*	Haydn	Euridice
1	September	Edinburgh	*Orfeo ed Euridice*	Haydn	Euridice
4	September	Edinburgh	*Orfeo ed Euridice*	Haydn	Euridice
6	September	Edinburgh	*Orfeo ed Euridice*	Haydn	Euridice
9	September	Edinburgh	*Orfeo ed Euridice*	Haydn	Euridice
29	October	London	Concert *Messiah*	Handel	
30	November	London	*Norma*	Bellini	Norma
4	December	London	*Norma*	Bellini	Norma
8	December	London	*Norma*	Bellini	Norma
12	December	London	*Norma*	Bellini	Norma
16	December	London	*Norma*	Bellini	Norma
21	December	London	*Norma*	Bellini	Norma
28	December	London	*Norma*	Bellini	Norma

—— 1968 ——

1	January	London	*Norma*	Bellini	Norma
7	January	London	Concert *Les Huguenots*	Meyerbeer	Marguerite de Valois

DATE		PLACE	PERFORMANCE	COMPOSER	ROLE
14	January	London	Recital		
7	February	New York	Concert *Orfeo ed Euridice*	Haydn	Euridice
10	February	New York	Concert *Orfeo ed Euridice*	Haydn	Euridice
13	February	Newark, New Jersey	Recital		
16	February	Philadelphia	Recital		
21	February	Salt Lake City	Concert		
29	February	New Orleans	*Lucia di Lammermoor*	Donizetti	Lucia
2	March	New Orleans	*Lucia di Lammermoor*	Donizetti	Lucia
9	March	Boston	*La Traviata*	Verdi	Violetta
11	March	Boston	*La Traviata*	Verdi	Violetta
13	March	Boston	*La Traviata*	Verdi	Violetta
16	March	New York	Metropolitan Opera Gala		
26	March	Philadelphia	*Norma*	Bellini	Norma
29	March	Philadelphia	*Norma*	Bellini	Norma
6	April	New York	Concert		
8	April	New York	Concert		
16	April	Seattle	*Don Giovanni*	Mozart	Donna Anna
18	April	Seattle	*Don Giovanni*	Mozart	Donna Anna
20	April	Seattle	*Don Giovanni*	Mozart	Donna Anna
24	April	Seattle	*Don Giovanni*	Mozart	Donna Anna
28	April	Toronto	Recital		
1	June	Florence	*Semiramide*	Rossini	Semiramide
4	June	Florence	*Semiramide*	Rossini	Semiramide
6	June	Florence	*Semiramide*	Rossini	Semiramide
9	June	Florence	*Semiramide*	Rossini	Semiramide
12	June	Florence	Recital		
10	July	London	Concert *Messiah*	Handel	
19	November	Philadelphia	*Lakmé*	Delibes	Lakmé
22	November	Philadelphia	*Lakmé*	Delibes	Lakmé
2	December	New York	*La Sonnambula*	Bellini	Amina
6	December	New York	*La Sonnambula*	Bellini	Amina
12	December	New York	*La Sonnambula*	Bellini	Amina
15	December	Boston	Concert		
18	December	New York	*La Sonnambula*	Bellini	Amina
21	December	New York	*La Sonnambula*	Bellini	Amina
24	December	New York	*La Sonnambula*	Bellini	Amina
28	December	New York	*La Sonnambula*	Bellini	Amina

──── 1969 ────

1	January	New York	*La Sonnambula*	Bellini	Amina
4	January	New York	*La Sonnambula*	Bellini	Amina
9	January	New York	*La Sonnambula*	Bellini	Amina
13	January	Columbia, South Carolina	Recital		
19	January	Indianapolis	Concert		
21	January	Warbash, Indiana	Concert		
29	January	Minneapolis	Recital		
9	February	London	Concert *Semiramide*	Rossini	Semiramide
19	February	London	Concert *Alcina*	Handel	Alcina
17	May	Buenos Aires	*La Traviata*	Verdi	Violetta
21	May	Buenos Aires	*La Traviata*	Verdi	Violetta
24	May	Buenos Aires	*La Traviata*	Verdi	Violetta
29	May	Buenos Aires	*La Traviata*	Verdi	Violetta
1	June	Buenos Aires	*La Traviata*	Verdi	Violetta
21	June	Buenos Aires	*Norma*	Bellini	Norma
24	June	Buenos Aires	*Norma*	Bellini	Norma
26	June	Buenos Aires	*Norma*	Bellini	Norma
29	June	Buenos Aires	*Norma*	Bellini	Norma
2	July	Buenos Aires	*Norma*	Bellini	Norma
8	July	Hollywood	Concert		
10	July	Portland, Oregon	Recital		
12	July	San Francisco	Recital		
17	July	Chicago	Concert		
20	July	Ottawa	Recital		
6	October	London	Recital		
11	October	The Hague	Concert		
9	November	Hamburg	*Giulio Cesare*	Handel	Cleopatra
12	November	Hamburg	*Giulio Cesare*	Handel	Cleopatra
15	November	Hamburg	*Giulio Cesare*	Handel	Cleopatra
19	November	Hamburg	*Giulio Cesare*	Handel	Cleopatra
23	November	Hamburg	*Giulio Cesare*	Handel	Cleopatra
27	November	Hamburg	*Giulio Cesare*	Handel	Cleopatra
6	December	Hamburg	*Giulio Cesare*	Handel	Cleopatra
10	December	Hamburg	*Giulio Cesare*	Handel	Cleopatra
16	December	Hamburg	*Giulio Cesare*	Handel	Cleopatra
21	December	Hamburg	*Giulio Cesare*	Handel	Cleopatra

DATE		PLACE	PERFORMANCE	COMPOSER	ROLE
— 1970 —					
24	January	Philadelphia	Gala Concert		
27	January	Ottawa	Recital		
30	January	Ann Arbor, Michigan	Recital		
8	February	Washington, DC	Recital		
30	February	London, Ontario	Recital		
3	March	New York	*Norma*	Bellini	Norma
6	March	New York	*Norma*	Bellini	Norma
10	March	New York	*Norma*	Bellini	Norma
14	March	New York	*Norma*	Bellini	Norma
19	March	New York	*Norma*	Bellini	Norma
23	March	New York	*Norma*	Bellini	Norma
27	March	New York	*Norma*	Bellini	Norma
4	April	New York	*Norma*	Bellini	Norma
9	April	New York	*Norma*	Bellini	Norma
11	April	New York	Metropolitan Opera Richard Tucker Gala		
14	April	New York	*Norma*	Bellini	Norma
18	April	New York	*Norma*	Bellini	Norma
22	April	Boston	*Norma*	Bellini	Norma
27	April	Philadelphia	*Norma*	Bellini	Norma
1	May	Cleveland, Ohio	*Norma*	Bellini	Norma
7	May	Atlanta	*Norma*	Bellini	Norma
12	May	Memphis	*Norma*	Bellini	Norma
16	May	Dallas	*Norma*	Bellini	Norma
20	May	Minneapolis	*Norma*	Bellini	Norma
23	May	University of California	Recital		
25	May	Winnipeg	Recital		
28	May	Detroit	*Norma*	Bellini	Norma
1	June	New York	*Lucia di Lammermoor*	Donizetti	Lucia
5	June	New York	*Lucia di Lammermoor*	Donizetti	Lucia
11	June	Bristol	Recital		
25	June	London	*Norma*	Bellini	Norma
29	June	London	*Norma*	Bellini	Norma
30	June	London	Royal Opera House David Webster Gala		
3	July	London	*Norma*	Bellini	Norma
7	July	London	*Norma*	Bellini	Norma
11	July	London	*Norma*	Bellini	Norma
7	September	New York	*Norma*	Bellini	Norma
23	September	New York	*Norma*	Bellini	Norma
28	September	New York	*Norma*	Bellini	Norma
3	October	New York	*Norma*	Bellini	Norma
7	October	New York	*Norma*	Bellini	Norma
12	October	New York	*La Traviata*	Verdi	Violetta
17	October	New York	*Norma*	Bellini	Norma
22	October	New York	*La Traviata*	Verdi	Violetta
27	October	New York	*La Traviata*	Verdi	Violetta
31	October	New York	*La Traviata*	Verdi	Violetta
12	**November**	**Seattle**	***Les Contes d'Hoffmann***	**Offenbach**	**Olympia, Giulietta, Antonia, Stella**
14	November	Seattle	*Les Contes d'Hoffmann*	Offenbach	Olympia, Giulietta, Antonia, Stella
18	November	Seattle	*Les Contes d'Hoffmann*	Offenbach	Olympia, Giulietta, Antonia, Stella
21	November	Seattle	*Les Contes d'Hoffmann*	Offenbach	Olympia, Giulietta, Antonia, Stella
2	December	New York	*La Traviata*	Verdi	Violetta
5	December	New York	*La Traviata*	Verdi	Violetta
10	December	New York	*Norma*	Bellini	Norma
14	December	New York	*Norma*	Bellini	Norma
19	December	New York	*Norma*	Bellini	Norma
— 1971 —					
28	January	Hamburg	*Giulio Cesare*	Handel	Cleopatra
31	January	Hamburg	*Giulio Cesare*	Handel	Cleopatra
9	February	Hamburg	*Giulio Cesare*	Handel	Cleopatra
12	February	Hamburg	*Giulio Cesare*	Handel	Cleopatra
17	February	Hamburg	*Giulio Cesare*	Handel	Cleopatra
7	March	Hamburg	*Lucia di Lammermoor*	Donizetti	Lucia
11	March	Hamburg	*Lucia di Lammermoor*	Donizetti	Lucia
14	March	Hamburg	*Lucia di Lammermoor*	Donizetti	Lucia
18	March	Hamburg	*Lucia di Lammermoor*	Donizetti	Lucia
21	March	Hamburg	*Lucia di Lammermoor*	Donizetti	Lucia
24	March	Hamburg	*Lucia di Lammermoor*	Donizetti	Lucia
27	March	Hamburg	*Lucia di Lammermoor*	Donizetti	Lucia
30	March	Hamburg	*Lucia di Lammermoor*	Donizetti	Lucia
3	April	Hamburg	*Lucia di Lammermoor*	Donizetti	Lucia
6	April	Hamburg	*Lucia di Lammermoor*	Donizetti	Lucia
12	April	Hamburg	*Lucia di Lammermoor*	Donizetti	Lucia

DATE		PLACE	PERFORMANCE	COMPOSER	ROLE
15	April	Hamburg	*Lucia di Lammermoor*	Donizetti	Lucia
18	April	Hamburg	*Lucia di Lammermoor*	Donizetti	Lucia
30	April	Geneva	Concert		
5	May	Madrid	Concert		
9	May	Liverpool	Recital		
14	May	Brighton	Concert *Rodelinda*	Handel	Rodelinda
16	May	Brighton	Concert *Rodelinda*	Handel	Rodelinda
23	May	London	Concert		
24	September	Chicago	*Semiramide*	Rossini	Semiramide
27	September	Chicago	*Semiramide*	Rossini	Semiramide
29	September	Chicago	*Semiramide*	Rossini	Semiramide
2	October	Chicago	*Semiramide*	Rossini	Semiramide
8	October	Chicago	*Semiramide*	Rossini	Semiramide
11	October	Chicago	*Semiramide*	Rossini	Semiramide
12	**November**	**San Francisco**	***Maria Stuarda***	**Donizetti**	**Maria**
16	November	San Francisco	*Maria Stuarda*	Donizetti	Maria
21	November	San Francisco	*Maria Stuarda*	Donizetti	Maria
24	November	San Francisco	*Maria Stuarda*	Donizetti	Maria
27	November	San Francisco	*Maria Stuarda*	Donizetti	Maria
30	November	Salt Lake City	Concert		
7	December	Philadelphia	*Lucia di Lammermoor*	Donizetti	Lucia
10	December	Philadelphia	*Lucia di Lammermoor*	Donizetti	Lucia
14	December	New Orleans	Concert		
17	December	Washington, DC	Recital		

—— 1972 ——

22	January	New York	Recital		
17	February	New York	*La Fille du Régiment*	Donizetti	Marie
23	February	New York	*La Fille du Régiment*	Donizetti	Marie
28	February	New York	*La Fille du Régiment*	Donizetti	Marie
4	March	New York	*La Fille du Régiment*	Donizetti	Marie
9	March	New York	*La Fille du Régiment*	Donizetti	Marie
14	March	New York	*La Fille du Régiment*	Donizetti	Marie
17	March	Raleigh, North Carolina	Recital		
18	March	Raleigh, North Carolina	Recital		
22	March	New York	*La Fille du Régiment*	Donizetti	Marie
25	March	New York	*La Fille du Régiment*	Donizetti	Marie
30	March	New York	*La Fille du Régiment*	Donizetti	Marie
7	April	New York	*La Fille du Régiment*	Donizetti	Marie
11	April	Philadelphia	Recital		
15	April	New York	*La Fille du Régiment*	Donizetti	Marie
18	April	New York	*La Fille du Régiment*	Donizetti	Marie
22	April	New York	Metropolitan Opera Rudolf Bing Gala		
24	April	Boston	*La Fille du Régiment*	Donizetti	Marie
2	May	Cleveland	*La Fille du Régiment*	Donizetti	Marie
5	May	Michigan	Recital		
8	May	Columbus, Ohio	Recital		
11	May	Atlanta, Georgia	*La Fille du Régiment*	Donizetti	Marie
17	May	Memphis	*La Fille du Régiment*	Donizetti	Marie
20	May	New Orleans	*La Fille du Régiment*	Donizetti	Marie
23	May	Minneapolis	*La Fille du Régiment*	Donizetti	Marie
3	June	Detroit	*La Fille du Régiment*	Donizetti	Marie
10	June	New York	*Rigoletto*	Verdi	Gilda
14	June	New York	*Rigoletto*	Verdi	Gilda
16	June	New Jersey	Concert		
19	June	New York	*Rigoletto*	Verdi	Gilda
22	June	New York	*Rigoletto*	Verdi	Gilda
11	September	San Francisco	Concert		
15	September	San Francisco	*Norma*	Bellini	Norma
20	September	San Francisco	*Norma*	Bellini	Norma
24	September	San Francisco	*Norma*	Bellini	Norma
30	September	San Francisco	*Norma*	Bellini	Norma
6	October	San Francisco	*Norma*	Bellini	Norma
26	**October**	**Vancouver**	***Lucrezia Borgia***	**Donizetti**	**Lucrezia**
28	October	Vancouver	*Lucrezia Borgia*	Donizetti	Lucrezia
1	November	Vancouver	*Lucrezia Borgia*	Donizetti	Lucrezia
4	November	Vancouver	*Lucrezia Borgia*	Donizetti	Lucrezia
8	November	Vancouver	*Lucrezia Borgia*	Donizetti	Lucrezia
11	November	Vancouver	*Lucrezia Borgia*	Donizetti	Lucrezia
17	November	Edmonton	*Lucrezia Borgia*	Donizetti	Lucrezia
20	November	Edmonton	*Lucrezia Borgia*	Donizetti	Lucrezia
22	November	Edmonton	*Lucrezia Borgia*	Donizetti	Lucrezia
31	December	New York	*La Fille du Régiment*	Donizetti	Marie

DATE		PLACE	PERFORMANCE	COMPOSER	ROLE
	1973				
6	January	New York	*La Fille du Régiment*	Donizetti	Marie
11	January	New York	*La Fille du Régiment*	Donizetti	Marie
15	January	New York	*La Fille du Régiment*	Donizetti	Marie
19	January	New York	*La Fille du Régiment*	Donizetti	Marie
22	January	New York	*La Fille du Régiment*	Donizetti	Marie
27	January	Ottawa	Recital		
31	January	Atlanta, Georgia	Recital		
3	February	Long Island, New York	Recital		
6	February	New Rochelle, New York	Recital		
10	February	New York	Metropolitan Opera Gala		
18	February	Cardiff	Recital		
23	February	London	Concert		
16	May	London	*Lucia di Lammermoor*	Donizetti	Lucia
19	May	London	*Lucia di Lammermoor*	Donizetti	Lucia
22	May	London	*Lucia di Lammermoor*	Donizetti	Lucia
25	May	London	*Lucia di Lammermoor*	Donizetti	Lucia
28	May	London	*Lucia di Lammermoor*	Donizetti	Lucia
31	May	London	*Lucia di Lammermoor*	Donizetti	Lucia
5	June	London	*Lucia di Lammermoor*	Donizetti	Lucia
9	June	London	*Lucia di Lammermoor*	Donizetti	Lucia
24	June	Scheveningen	*Rodelinda*	Handel	Rodelinda
27	June	Rotterdam	*Rodelinda*	Handel	Rodelinda
30	June	Amsterdam	*Rodelinda*	Handel	Rodelinda
3	July	Amsterdam	*Rodelinda*	Handel	Rodelinda
8	**September**	**San Francisco**	***Die Fledermaus***	**J Strauss**	**Rosalinde**
11	September	San Francisco	*Die Fledermaus*	J Strauss	Rosalinde
14	September	San Francisco	*Die Fledermaus*	J Strauss	Rosalinde
19	September	San Francisco	*Die Fledermaus*	J Strauss	Rosalinde
26	September	Claremont, California	Recital		
30	September	San Francisco	*Die Fledermaus*	J Strauss	Rosalinde
2	October	San Francisco	*Die Fledermaus*	J Strauss	Rosalinde
5	October	Fresno, California	Recital		
20	October	Chicago	*La Fille du Régiment*	Donizetti	Marie
24	October	Chicago	*La Fille du Régiment*	Donizetti	Marie
26	October	Chicago	*La Fille du Régiment*	Donizetti	Marie
2	November	Chicago	*La Fille du Régiment*	Donizetti	Marie
5	November	Chicago	*La Fille du Régiment*	Donizetti	Marie
7	November	Chicago	*La Fille du Régiment*	Donizetti	Marie
29	November	New York	*Les Contes d'Hoffmann*	Offenbach	Olympia, Giulietta, Antonia, Stella
3	December	New York	*Les Contes d'Hoffmann*	Offenbach	Olympia, Giulietta, Antonia, Stella
8	December	New York	*Les Contes d'Hoffmann*	Offenbach	Olympia, Giulietta, Antonia, Stella
11	December	New York	*Les Contes d'Hoffmann*	Offenbach	Olympia, Giulietta, Antonia, Stella
14	December	New York	*Les Contes d'Hoffmann*	Offenbach	Olympia, Giulietta, Antonia, Stella
16	December	Brooklyn, New York	Recital		
19	December	New York	*Les Contes d'Hoffmann*	Offenbach	Olympia, Giulietta, Antonia, Stella
22	December	New York	*Les Contes d'Hoffmann*	Offenbach	Olympia, Giulietta, Antonia, Stella
	1974				
17	January	New York	*Les Contes d'Hoffmann*	Offenbach	Olympia, Giulietta, Antonia, Stella
21	January	New York	*Les Contes d'Hoffmann*	Offenbach	Olympia, Giulietta, Antonia, Stella
25	January	New York	*Les Contes d'Hoffmann*	Offenbach	Olympia, Giulietta, Antonia, Stella
2	February	New York	*Les Contes d'Hoffmann*	Offenbach	Olympia, Giulietta, Antonia, Stella
9	February	Miami	*Lucia di Lammermoor*	Donizetti	Lucia
13	February	Miami Beach	*Lucia di Lammermoor*	Donizetti	Lucia
16	February	Miami	*Lucia di Lammermoor*	Donizetti	Lucia
19	February	Fort Lauderdale, Florida	*Lucia di Lammermoor*	Donizetti	Lucia
26	February	Philadelphia	*Maria Stuarda*	Donizetti	Maria
1	March	Philadelphia	*Maria Stuarda*	Donizetti	Maria
4	March	Hartford, Connecticut	*Maria Stuarda*	Donizetti	Maria
18	April	Lisbon	*La Traviata*	Verdi	Violetta
21	April	Lisbon	*La Traviata*	Verdi	Violetta
24	April	Lisbon	*La Traviata*	Verdi	Violetta
4	May	Detroit	*Les Contes d'Hoffmann*	Offenbach	Olympia, Giulietta, Antonia, Stella
7	May	Atlanta, Georgia	*Les Contes d'Hoffmann*	Offenbach	Olympia, Giulietta, Antonia, Stella
10	May	Alabama	Recital		
13	May	Memphis	*Les Contes d'Hoffmann*	Offenbach	Olympia, Giulietta, Antonia, Stella
16	May	Dallas	*Les Contes d'Hoffmann*	Offenbach	Olympia, Giulietta, Antonia, Stella
20	May	Minneapolis	*Les Contes d'Hoffmann*	Offenbach	Olympia, Giulietta, Antonia, Stella
23	May	Kansas City	Recital		
27	May	New York	*Les Contes d'Hoffmann*	Offenbach	Olympia, Giulietta, Antonia, Stella
30	May	New York	*Les Contes d'Hoffmann*	Offenbach	Olympia, Giulietta, Antonia, Stella
6	July	Sydney	Recital		
13	July	Sydney	*Les Contes d'Hoffmann*	Offenbach	Olympia, Giulietta, Antonia, Stella

DATE		PLACE	PERFORMANCE	COMPOSER	ROLE
16	July	Sydney	*Les Contes d'Hoffmann*	Offenbach	Olympia, Giulietta, Antonia, Stella
19	July	Sydney	*Les Contes d'Hoffmann*	Offenbach	Olympia, Giulietta, Antonia, Stella
24	July	Sydney	*Les Contes d'Hoffmann*	Offenbach	Olympia, Giulietta, Antonia, Stella
27	July	Sydney	*Les Contes d'Hoffmann*	Offenbach	Olympia, Giulietta, Antonia, Stella
30	July	Sydney	*Les Contes d'Hoffmann*	Offenbach	Olympia, Giulietta, Antonia, Stella
2	August	Sydney	*Les Contes d'Hoffmann*	Offenbach	Olympia, Giulietta, Antonia, Stella
6	August	Sydney	*Les Contes d'Hoffmann*	Offenbach	Olympia, Giulietta, Antonia, Stella
9	August	Sydney	Recital		
13	August	Melbourne	Recital		
17	August	Melbourne	Recital		
23	**October**	**San Francisco**	***Esclarmonde***	**Massenet**	**Esclarmonde**
26	October	San Francisco	*Esclarmonde*	Massenet	Esclarmonde
29	October	San Francisco	*Esclarmonde*	Massenet	Esclarmonde
2	November	San Francisco	*Esclarmonde*	Massenet	Esclarmonde
4	November	Sacramento, California	Recital		
8	November	San Francisco	*Esclarmonde*	Massenet	Esclarmonde
13	November	Vancouver	Recital		
23	November	Phoenix	*Lucia di Lammermoor*	Donizetti	Lucia
26	November	Phoenix	*Lucia di Lammermoor*	Donizetti	Lucia
4	December	San Diego	*Lucia di Lammermoor*	Donizetti	Lucia
6	December	San Diego	*Lucia di Lammermoor*	Donizetti	Lucia
8	December	San Diego	*Lucia di Lammermoor*	Donizetti	Lucia

—— 1975 ——

DATE		PLACE	PERFORMANCE	COMPOSER	ROLE
6	January	London	*La Traviata*	Verdi	Violetta
11	January	London	*La Traviata*	Verdi	Violetta
16	January	London	*La Traviata*	Verdi	Violetta
19	January	Manchester	Recital		
21	January	London	*La Traviata*	Verdi	Violetta
24	January	London	*La Traviata*	Verdi	Violetta
25	January	London	Darwin Gala		
27	January	London	La Traviata	Verdi	Violetta
29	January	Stratford-upon-Avon	Recital		
18	February	Rochester, New York	Recital		
18	March	Ithaca, New York	Recital		
25	March	Philadelphia	*La Traviata*	Verdi	Violetta
27	March	Philadelphia	*La Traviata*	Verdi	Violetta
8	April	Houston	*Lucrezia Borgia*	Donizetti	Lucrezia
11	April	Houston	*Lucrezia Borgia*	Donizetti	Lucrezia
13	April	Houston	*Lucrezia Borgia*	Donizetti	Lucrezia
29	April	Las Palmas	*Maria Stuarda*	Donizetti	Maria
2	May	Las Palmas	*Maria Stuarda*	Donizetti	Maria
29	May	Japan	*La Traviata*	Verdi	Violetta
3	June	Japan	*La Traviata*	Verdi	Violetta
6	June	Japan	*La Traviata*	Verdi	Violetta
9	June	Japan	*La Traviata*	Verdi	Violetta
12	June	Japan	*La Traviata*	Verdi	Violetta
12	**September**	**San Francisco**	***Il Trovatore***	**Verdi**	**Leonora**
17	September	San Francisco	*Il Trovatore*	Verdi	Leonora
21	September	San Francisco	*Il Trovatore*	Verdi	Leonora
23	September	San Diego	Recital		
27	September	San Francisco	*Il Trovatore*	Verdi	Leonora
30	September	San Francisco	*Il Trovatore*	Verdi	Leonora
3	October	San Francisco	*Il Trovatore*	Verdi	Leonora
5	October	Pasadena, California	Recital		
12	November	Chicago	*Lucia di Lammermoor*	Donizetti	Lucia
15	November	Chicago	*Lucia di Lammermoor*	Donizetti	Lucia
18	November	Chicago	*Lucia di Lammermoor*	Donizetti	Lucia
21	November	Chicago	*Lucia di Lammermoor*	Donizetti	Lucia
24	November	Chicago	*Lucia di Lammermoor*	Donizetti	Lucia
28	November	Chicago	*Lucia di Lammermoor*	Donizetti	Lucia
1	December	Chicago	*Lucia di Lammermoor*	Donizetti	Lucia
4	December	Chicago	*Lucia di Lammermoor*	Donizetti	Lucia

—— 1976 ——

DATE		PLACE	PERFORMANCE	COMPOSER	ROLE
25	January	New York	*I Puritani*	Bellini	Elvira
28	January	New York	*I Puritani*	Bellini	Elvira
2	February	New York	*I Puritani*	Bellini	Elvira
5	February	New York	*I Puritani*	Bellini	Elvira
9	February	New York	*I Puritani*	Bellini	Elvira
13	February	New York	*I Puritani*	Bellini	Elvira
17	February	New York	*I Puritani*	Bellini	Elvira
20	February	New York	*I Puritani*	Bellini	Elvira
25	February	New York	*I Puritani*	Bellini	Elvira
29	February	New York	*I Puritani*	Bellini	Elvira

DATE		PLACE	PERFORMANCE	COMPOSER	ROLE
22	**April**	**Vancouver**	***The Merry Widow***	**Lehar**	**Anna Glawari**
24	April	Vancouver	*The Merry Widow*	Lehar	Anna Glawari
27	April	Vancouver	*The Merry Widow*	Lehar	Anna Glawari
29	April	Vancouver	*The Merry Widow*	Lehar	Anna Glawari
1	May	Vancouver	*The Merry Widow*	Lehar	Anna Glawari
4	May	Vancouver	*The Merry Widow*	Lehar	Anna Glawari
19	May	Wellington	Concert		
22	May	Wellington	Concert		
25	May	Hamilton	Concert		
29	May	Hamilton	Concert		
1	June	Napier	Recital		
4	June	Christchurch	Concert		
7	June	Wellington	Recital		
10	June	Auckland	Concert		
13	June	Auckland	Concert		
16	June	Christchurch	Recital		
10	July	Sydney	*Lakmé*	Delibes	Lakmé
14	July	Sydney	*Lakmé*	Delibes	Lakmé
17	July	Sydney	*Lakmé*	Delibes	Lakmé
21	July	Sydney	*Lakmé*	Delibes	Lakmé
24	July	Sydney	*Lakmé*	Delibes	Lakmé
26	July	Sydney	*Lakmé*	Delibes	Lakmé
30	July	Sydney	*Lakmé*	Delibes	Lakmé
2	August	Sydney	*Lakmé*	Delibes	Lakmé
6	August	Sydney	*Lakmé*	Delibes	Lakmé
8	August	Sydney	Recital		
13	August	Sydney	*Lakmé*	Delibes	Lakmé
18	August	Sydney	*Lakmé*	Delibes	Lakmé
21	August	Adelaide	Recital		
24	August	Adelaide	Recital		
27	August	Canberra	Recital		
29	October	Seattle	Recital		
31	October	Winnipeg	Recital		
19	November	New York	*Esclarmonde*	Massenet	Esclarmonde
24	November	New York	*Esclarmonde*	Massenet	Esclarmonde
27	November	New York	*Esclarmonde*	Massenet	Esclarmonde
1	December	New York	*Esclarmonde*	Massenet	Esclarmonde
4	December	New York	*Esclarmonde*	Massenet	Esclarmonde
7	December	New York	*Esclarmonde*	Massenet	Esclarmonde
11	December	New York	*Esclarmonde*	Massenet	Esclarmonde
12	December	New York	United Nations Concert		
17	December	New York	*Esclarmonde*	Massenet	Esclarmonde
20	December	New York	*Esclarmonde*	Massenet	Esclarmonde

—— 1977 ——

22	January	Ames, Iowa	Recital		
25	January	Buffalo, New York	Recital		
27	January	Akron, Ohio	Recital		
29	January	Danville, Kentucky	Recital		
1	February	Sarasota, Florida	Recital		
3	February	Miami	Recital		
9	February	Puerto Rico	*Lucia di Lammermoor*	Donizetti	Lucia
11	February	Puerto Rico	*Lucia di Lammermoor*	Donizetti	Lucia
10	March	Scheveningen	*Maria Stuarda*	Donizetti	Maria
12	March	Rotterdam	*Maria Stuarda*	Donizetti	Maria
13	March	Amsterdam	Recital		
15	March	Scheveningen	*Maria Stuarda*	Donizetti	Maria
18	March	Utrecht	*Maria Stuarda*	Donizetti	Maria
22	March	Amsterdam	*Maria Stuarda*	Donizetti	Maria
25	March	Eindhoven	*Maria Stuarda*	Donizetti	Maria
27	March	Amsterdam	*Maria Stuarda*	Donizetti	Maria
30	March	Amsterdam	*Maria Stuarda*	Donizetti	Maria
7	June	Sydney	*Lucrezia Borgia*	Donizetti	Lucrezia
11	June	Sydney	*Lucrezia Borgia*	Donizetti	Lucrezia
14	June	Sydney	*Lucrezia Borgia*	Donizetti	Lucrezia
18	June	Sydney	*Lucrezia Borgia*	Donizetti	Lucrezia
22	June	Sydney	*Lucrezia Borgia*	Donizetti	Lucrezia
25	June	Sydney	*Lucrezia Borgia*	Donizetti	Lucrezia
28	June	Sydney	*Lucrezia Borgia*	Donizetti	Lucrezia
5	July	Sydney	*Lucrezia Borgia*	Donizetti	Lucrezia
8	July	Sydney	*Lucrezia Borgia*	Donizetti	Lucrezia
16	**July**	**Sydney**	***Suor Angelica***	**Puccini**	**Suor Angelica**
19	July	Sydney	*Suor Angelica*	Puccini	Suor Angelica
22	July	Sydney	*Suor Angelica*	Puccini	Suor Angelica
24	July	Sydney	Opera in Concert		

DATE		PLACE	PERFORMANCE	COMPOSER	ROLE
26	July	Sydney	*Suor Angelica*	Puccini	Suor Angelica
23	**September**	**Vancouver**	***Le Roi de Lahore***	**Massenet**	**Sita**
25	September	Vancouver	*Le Roi de Lahore*	Massenet	Sita
28	September	Vancouver	*Le Roi de Lahore*	Massenet	Sita
1	October	Vancouver	*Le Roi de Lahore*	Massenet	Sita
7	October	Vancouver	*Don Giovanni*	Mozart	Donna Anna
9	October	Vancouver	*Le Roi de Lahore*	Massenet	Sita
12	October	Vancouver	*Don Giovanni*	Mozart	Donna Anna
14	October	Vancouver	*Don Giovanni*	Mozart	Donna Anna
16	October	Vancouver	*Don Giovanni*	Mozart	Donna Anna
22	October	Vancouver	*Don Giovanni*	Mozart	Donna Anna
27	October	Seattle	*Le Roi de Lahore*	Massenet	Sita
29	October	Seattle	*Le Roi de Lahore*	Massenet	Sita
2	November	Seattle	*Le Roi de Lahore*	Massenet	Sita
5	November	Seattle	*Le Roi de Lahore*	Massenet	Sita
15	December	London	*Maria Stuarda*	Donizetti	Maria
20	December	London	*Maria Stuarda*	Donizetti	Maria
23	December	London	*Maria Stuarda*	Donizetti	Maria
26	December	London	*Maria Stuarda*	Donizetti	Maria
29	December	London	*Maria Stuarda*	Donizetti	Maria

───── 1978 ─────

DATE		PLACE	PERFORMANCE	COMPOSER	ROLE
19	January	Sydney	*The Merry Widow*	Lehar	Anna Glawari
21	January	Sydney	*The Merry Widow*	Lehar	Anna Glawari
23	January	Sydney	*The Merry Widow*	Lehar	Anna Glawari
25	January	Sydney	*The Merry Widow*	Lehar	Anna Glawari
26	January	Sydney	*The Merry Widow*	Lehar	Anna Glawari
28	January	Sydney	*The Merry Widow*	Lehar	Anna Glawari
31	January	Sydney	*The Merry Widow*	Lehar	Anna Glawari
2	February	Sydney	*The Merry Widow*	Lehar	Anna Glawari
4	February	Sydney	*The Merry Widow*	Lehar	Anna Glawari
6	February	Sydney	*The Merry Widow*	Lehar	Anna Glawari
8	February	Sydney	*The Merry Widow*	Lehar	Anna Glawari
9	February	Sydney	*The Merry Widow*	Lehar	Anna Glawari
11	February	Sydney	*The Merry Widow*	Lehar	Anna Glawari
18	February	Sydney	Opera in Concert		
10	March	New York	*Don Giovanni*	Mozart	Donna Anna
16	March	New York	*Don Giovanni*	Mozart	Donna Anna
18	March	New York	*Don Giovanni*	Mozart	Donna Anna
21	March	New York	*Don Giovanni*	Mozart	Donna Anna
25	March	New York	*Don Giovanni*	Mozart	Donna Anna
27	March	New York	*Don Giovanni*	Mozart	Donna Anna
30	March	New York	*Don Giovanni*	Mozart	Donna Anna
4	April	Kalamazoo, Michigan	Recital		
7	April	Salt Lake City	Recital		
9	April	Minneapolis	Recital		
12	April	Memphis	Recital		
14	April	Tulsa, Oklahoma	Recital		
15	April	New Orleans	Recital		
7	June	Tokyo	Recital		
10	June	Nagoya	Recital		
13	June	Seoul	Recital		
5	July	Sydney	*Norma*	Bellini	Norma
8	July	Sydney	*Norma*	Bellini	Norma
11	July	Sydney	*Norma*	Bellini	Norma
14	July	Sydney	*Norma*	Bellini	Norma
17	July	Sydney	*Norma*	Bellini	Norma
20	July	Sydney	*Norma*	Bellini	Norma
26	July	Sydney	*Norma*	Bellini	Norma
29	July	Sydney	*Norma*	Bellini	Norma
1	August	Sydney	*Norma*	Bellini	Norma
4	August	Sydney	*Norma*	Bellini	Norma
10	August	Sydney	*Norma*	Bellini	Norma
13	August	Sydney	Recital		
23	August	Sydney	*Norma*	Bellini	Norma
26	August	Sydney	*Norma*	Bellini	Norma
26	November	London	Concert		
14	December	Amsterdam	*Norma*	Bellini	Norma
17	December	Amsterdam	*Norma*	Bellini	Norma
20	December	Amsterdam	*Norma*	Bellini	Norma
23	December	Scheveningen	*Norma*	Bellini	Norma
26	December	Scheveningen	*Norma*	Bellini	Norma
29	December	Rotterdam	*Norma*	Bellini	Norma

DATE		PLACE	PERFORMANCE	COMPOSER	ROLE
	1979				
1	January	Utrecht	*Norma*	Bellini	Norma
11	January	Philadelphia	Recital		
14	January	Toronto	Recital		
22	January	New York	Concert		
9	February	Sydney	*The Merry Widow*	Lehar	Anna Glawari
12	February	Sydney	*The Merry Widow*	Lehar	Anna Glawari
14	February	Sydney	*The Merry Widow*	Lehar	Anna Glawari
16	February	Sydney	*The Merry Widow*	Lehar	Anna Glawari
19	February	Sydney	*The Merry Widow*	Lehar	Anna Glawari
22	February	Sydney	*The Merry Widow*	Lehar	Anna Glawari
24	February	Sydney	*The Merry Widow*	Lehar	Anna Glawari
28	February	Sydney	*The Merry Widow*	Lehar	Anna Glawari
2	March	Sydney	*The Merry Widow*	Lehar	Anna Glawari
10	March	Melbourne	*La Traviata*	Verdi	Violetta
13	March	Melbourne	*La Traviata*	Verdi	Violetta
16	March	Melbourne	*La Traviata*	Verdi	Violetta
19	March	Melbourne	*La Traviata*	Verdi	Violetta
24	March	Melbourne	*La Traviata*	Verdi	Violetta
31	March	Brisbane	*Norma*	Bellini	Norma
3	April	Brisbane	*Norma*	Bellini	Norma
6	April	Brisbane	*Norma*	Bellini	Norma
9	April	Brisbane	*Norma*	Bellini	Norma
26	April	Paris	Recital		
29	April	Munich	Recital		
6	May	Stockholm	Concert *Lucia di Lammermoor*	Donizetti	Lucia
14	May	Asolo	Recital		
4	**July**	**Sydney**	**Idomeneo**	**Mozart**	**Elettra**
7	July	Sydney	*Idomeneo*	Mozart	Elettra
10	July	Sydney	*La Traviata*	Verdi	Violetta
14	July	Sydney	*Idomeneo*	Mozart	Elettra
17	July	Sydney	*Idomeneo*	Mozart	Elettra
20	July	Sydney	*Idomeneo*	Mozart	Elettra
25	July	Sydney	*Idomeneo*	Mozart	Elettra
28	July	Sydney	*Idomeneo*	Mozart	Elettra
4	August	Melbourne	*Don Giovanni*	Mozart	Donna Anna
7	August	Melbourne	*Don Giovanni*	Mozart	Donna Anna
10	August	Melbourne	*Don Giovanni*	Mozart	Donna Anna
13	August	Melbourne	*Don Giovanni*	Mozart	Donna Anna
16	August	Melbourne	*Don Giovanni*	Mozart	Donna Anna
18	August	Melbourne	*Don Giovanni*	Mozart	Donna Anna
16	September	Glasgow	Recital		
4	October	Ann Arbor, Michigan	Recital		
7	October	Cincinnatti	Recital		
15	October	New York	Concert		
22	November	Adelaide	*The Merry Widow*	Lehar	Anna Glawari
26	November	Adelaide	*The Merry Widow*	Lehar	Anna Glawari
28	November	Adelaide	*The Merry Widow*	Lehar	Anna Glawari
30	November	Adelaide	*The Merry Widow*	Lehar	Anna Glawari
2	December	Adelaide	Opera in Concert		
6	December	Melbourne	*The Merry Widow*	Lehar	Anna Glawari
8	December	Melbourne	*The Merry Widow*	Lehar	Anna Glawari
10	December	Melbourne	*The Merry Widow*	Lehar	Anna Glawari
12	December	Melbourne	*The Merry Widow*	Lehar	Anna Glawari
13	December	Melbourne	*The Merry Widow*	Lehar	Anna Glawari
15	December	Melbourne	*The Merry Widow*	Lehar	Anna Glawari
	1980				
26	January	Sydney	Opera in Concert		
6	February	Sydney	*Lucia di Lammermoor*	Donizetti	Lucia
9	February	Sydney	*Lucia di Lammermoor*	Donizetti	Lucia
12	February	Sydney	*Lucia di Lammermoor*	Donizetti	Lucia
15	February	Sydney	*Lucia di Lammermoor*	Donizetti	Lucia
20	February	Sydney	*Lucia di Lammermoor*	Donizetti	Lucia
23	February	Sydney	*Lucia di Lammermoor*	Donizetti	Lucia
26	February	Sydney	*Lucia di Lammermoor*	Donizetti	Lucia
29	February	Sydney	*Lucia di Lammermoor*	Donizetti	Lucia
26	March	London	*Lucrezia Borgia*	Donizetti	Lucrezia
29	March	London	*Lucrezia Borgia*	Donizetti	Lucrezia
1	April	London	*Lucrezia Borgia*	Donizetti	Lucrezia
5	April	London	*Lucrezia Borgia*	Donizetti	Lucrezia
9	April	London	*Lucrezia Borgia*	Donizetti	Lucrezia
12	April	London	*Lucrezia Borgia*	Donizetti	Lucrezia
16	April	London	*Lucrezia Borgia*	Donizetti	Lucrezia
21	April	Stuttgart	Recital		

DATE		PLACE	PERFORMANCE	COMPOSER	ROLE
24	April	Vienna	Recital		
15	May	Rome	*Lucrezia Borgia*	Donizetti	Lucrezia
18	May	Rome	*Lucrezia Borgia*	Donizetti	Lucrezia
21	May	Rome	*Lucrezia Borgia*	Donizetti	Lucrezia
24	May	Rome	*Lucrezia Borgia*	Donizetti	Lucrezia
28	May	Rome	*Lucrezia Borgia*	Donizetti	Lucrezia
31	May	Rome	*Lucrezia Borgia*	Donizetti	Lucrezia
3	June	Rome	*Lucrezia Borgia*	Donizetti	Lucrezia
2	**July**	**Sydney**	***I Masnadieri***	**Verdi**	**Amalia**
5	July	Sydney	*I Masnadieri*	Verdi	Amalia
8	July	Sydney	*I Masnadieri*	Verdi	Amalia
11	July	Sydney	*I Masnadieri*	Verdi	Amalia
17	July	Sydney	*I Masnadieri*	Verdi	Amalia
23	July	Sydney	*I Masnadieri*	Verdi	Amalia
26	July	Sydney	*I Masnadieri*	Verdi	Amalia
29	July	Sydney	*I Masnadieri*	Verdi	Amalia
2	August	Sydney	*I Masnadieri*	Verdi	Amalia
5	August	Sydney	*I Masnadieri*	Verdi	Amalia
9	August	Sydney	*I Masnadieri*	Verdi	Amalia
22	August	Sydney	*Lucia di Lammermoor*	Donizetti	Lucia
25	August	Sydney	*Lucia di Lammermoor*	Donizetti	Lucia
28	August	Sydney	*Lucia di Lammermoor*	Donizetti	Lucia
31	August	Sydney	*Lucia di Lammermoor*	Donizetti	Lucia
3	September	Sydney	*Lucia di Lammermoor*	Donizetti	Lucia
6	September	Sydney	*Lucia di Lammermoor*	Donizetti	Lucia
5	October	San Diego	*Die Fledermaus*	J Strauss	Rosalinde
8	October	San Diego	*Die Fledermaus*	J Strauss	Rosalinde
11	October	San Diego	*Die Fledermaus*	J Strauss	Rosalinde
16	October	San Diego	*Die Fledermaus*	J Strauss	Rosalinde
19	October	San Diego	*Die Fledermaus*	J Strauss	Rosalinde
5	November	Melbourne	*Lucia di Lammermoor*	Donizetti	Lucia
8	November	Melbourne	*Lucia di Lammermoor*	Donizetti	Lucia
11	November	Melbourne	*Lucia di Lammermoor*	Donizetti	Lucia
14	November	Melbourne	*Lucia di Lammermoor*	Donizetti	Lucia
19	November	Adelaide	*Lucia di Lammermoor*	Donizetti	Lucia
22	November	Adelaide	*Lucia di Lammermoor*	Donizetti	Lucia
26	November	Adelaide	*Lucia di Lammermoor*	Donizetti	Lucia
29	November	Adelaide	*Lucia di Lammermoor*	Donizetti	Lucia

—— 1981 ——————————————————————————————————

DATE		PLACE	PERFORMANCE	COMPOSER	ROLE
28	January	Sydney	*Otello*	Verdi	Desdemona
31	January	Sydney	*Otello*	Verdi	Desdemona
3	February	Sydney	*Otello*	Verdi	Desdemona
6	February	Sydney	*Otello*	Verdi	Desdemona
9	February	Sydney	*Otello*	Verdi	Desdemona
12	February	Sydney	*Otello*	Verdi	Desdemona
17	February	Sydney	*Otello*	Verdi	Desdemona
20	February	Sydney	*Otello*	Verdi	Desdemona
23	February	Sydney	*Otello*	Verdi	Desdemona
28	February	Sydney	*Otello*	Verdi	Desdemona
20	March	New York	Concert		
23	March	New York	Concert		
27	March	Pittsburgh	Concert		
4	April	Memphis	*La Traviata*	Verdi	Violetta
7	April	Rock Hill, South Carolina	Concert		
11	April	Brooklyn, New York	Concert		
28	April	Toronto	*Norma*	Bellini	Norma
1	May	Toronto	*Norma*	Bellini	Norma
4	May	Toronto	*Norma*	Bellini	Norma
7	May	Toronto	*Norma*	Bellini	Norma
10	May	Toronto	*Norma*	Bellini	Norma
20	May	Melbourne	*Otello*	Verdi	Desdemona
23	May	Melbourne	*Otello*	Verdi	Desdemona
26	May	Melbourne	*Otello*	Verdi	Desdemona
29	May	Melbourne	*Otello*	Verdi	Desdemona
1	June	Melbourne	*Otello*	Verdi	Desdemona
4	June	Melbourne	*Otello*	Verdi	Desdemona
17	June	Sydney	*La Traviata*	Verdi	Violetta
20	June	Sydney	*La Traviata*	Verdi	Violetta
24	June	Sydney	*La Traviata*	Verdi	Violetta
27	June	Sydney	*La Traviata*	Verdi	Violetta
30	June	Sydney	*La Traviata*	Verdi	Violetta
4	July	Sydney	*La Traviata*	Verdi	Violetta
9	July	Sydney	*La Traviata*	Verdi	Violetta
24	July	Sydney	*Les Huguenots*	Meyerbeer	Marguerite de Valois

DATE		PLACE	PERFORMANCE	COMPOSER	ROLE
27	July	Sydney	*Les Huguenots*	Meyerbeer	Marguerite de Valois
31	July	Sydney	*Les Huguenots*	Meyerbeer	Marguerite de Valois
5	August	Sydney	*Les Huguenots*	Meyerbeer	Marguerite de Valois
8	August	Sydney	*Les Huguenots*	Meyerbeer	Marguerite de Valois
11	August	Sydney	*Les Huguenots*	Meyerbeer	Marguerite de Valois
15	August	Sydney	*Les Huguenots*	Meyerbeer	Marguerite de Valois
18	August	Sydney	*Les Huguenots*	Meyerbeer	Marguerite de Valois
22	August	Sydney	*Les Huguenots*	Meyerbeer	Marguerite de Valois
3	October	San Francisco	*The Merry Widow*	Lehar	Anna Glawari
6	October	San Francisco	*The Merry Widow*	Lehar	Anna Glawari
9	October	San Francisco	*The Merry Widow*	Lehar	Anna Glawari
13	October	San Francisco	*The Merry Widow*	Lehar	Anna Glawari
16	October	San Francisco	*The Merry Widow*	Lehar	Anna Glawari
18	October	San Diego	Concert		
21	October	San Francisco	*The Merry Widow*	Lehar	Anna Glawari
25	October	San Francisco	*The Merry Widow*	Lehar	Anna Glawari
28	October	San Francisco	*The Merry Widow*	Lehar	Anna Glawari
31	October	San Francisco	*The Merry Widow*	Lehar	Anna Glawari
4	November	Washington, DC	George London Tribute Concert		
29	November	London	Concert		
10	December	London	*Il Trovatore*	Verdi	Leonora
14	December	London	*Il Trovatore*	Verdi	Leonora
18	December	London	*Il Trovatore*	Verdi	Leonora
22	December	London	*Il Trovatore*	Verdi	Leonora
	—— 1982 ——				
1	January	London	*Il Trovatore*	Verdi	Leonora
4	January	London	*Il Trovatore*	Verdi	Leonora
18	January	Sydney	Park Concert *La Traviata*	Verdi	Violetta
3	February	Sydney	*Lucrezia Borgia*	Donizetti	Lucrezia
6	February	Sydney	*Lucrezia Borgia*	Donizetti	Lucrezia
10	February	Sydney	*Lucrezia Borgia*	Donizetti	Lucrezia
17	February	Sydney	*Lucrezia Borgia*	Donizetti	Lucrezia
20	February	Sydney	*Lucrezia Borgia*	Donizetti	Lucrezia
23	February	Sydney	*Lucrezia Borgia*	Donizetti	Lucrezia
1	March	Sydney	*Lucrezia Borgia*	Donizetti	Lucrezia
4	March	Sydney	*Lucrezia Borgia*	Donizetti	Lucrezia
9	March	Perth	Recital		
26	March	Stockholm	Concert *Lucrezia Borgia*	Donizetti	Lucrezia
9	April	Venice	Recital		
12	April	Genoa	Recital		
29	April	Amsterdam	*Lucia di Lammermoor*	Donizetti	Lucia
2	May	Amsterdam	*Lucia di Lammermoor*	Donizetti	Lucia
8	May	Scheveningen	*Lucia di Lammermoor*	Donizetti	Lucia
11	May	Scheveningen	*Lucia di Lammermoor*	Donizetti	Lucia
14	May	Utrecht	*Lucia di Lammermoor*	Donizetti	Lucia
17	May	Eindhoven	*Lucia di Lammermoor*	Donizetti	Lucia
20	May	Rotterdam	*Lucia di Lammermoor*	Donizetti	Lucia
24	May	Amsterdam	*Lucia di Lammermoor*	Donizetti	Lucia
27	May	Amsterdam	*Lucia di Lammermoor*	Donizetti	Lucia
25	June	Sydney	*Die Fledermaus*	J Strauss	Rosalinde
28	June	Sydney	*Die Fledermaus*	J Strauss	Rosalinde
3	July	Sydney	*Die Fledermaus*	J Strauss	Rosalinde
6	July	Sydney	*Die Fledermaus*	J Strauss	Rosalinde
10	July	Sydney	*Die Fledermaus*	J Strauss	Rosalinde
13	July	Sydney	*Die Fledermaus*	J Strauss	Rosalinde
16	July	Sydney	*Die Fledermaus*	J Strauss	Rosalinde
19	July	Sydney	*Die Fledermaus*	J Strauss	Rosalinde
22	July	Sydney	*Die Fledermaus*	J Strauss	Rosalinde
25	July	Sydney	Concert		
28	July	Sydney	*Die Fledermaus*	J Strauss	Rosalinde
31	July	Sydney	*Die Fledermaus*	J Strauss	Rosalinde
4	August	Sydney	*Die Fledermaus*	J Strauss	Rosalinde
11	September	San Francisco	*Norma*	Bellini	Norma
14	September	San Francisco	*Norma*	Bellini	Norma
17	September	San Francisco	*Norma*	Bellini	Norma
21	September	San Francisco	*Norma*	Bellini	Norma
26	September	San Francisco	*Norma*	Bellini	Norma
29	September	San Francisco	*Norma*	Bellini	Norma
2	October	San Francisco	*Norma*	Bellini	Norma
17	October	London	Royal Opera House 30th Anniversary Concert		
24	October	New York	Concert		
1	November	New York	*Lucia di Lammermoor*	Donizetti	Lucia
5	November	New York	*Lucia di Lammermoor*	Donizetti	Lucia
10	November	New York	*Lucia di Lammermoor*	Donizetti	Lucia

DATE		PLACE	PERFORMANCE	COMPOSER	ROLE
13	November	New York	*Lucia di Lammermoor*	Donizetti	Lucia
20	November	New York	*Lucia di Lammermoor*	Donizetti	Lucia
24	November	New York	*Lucia di Lammermoor*	Donizetti	Lucia
27	November	New York	*Lucia di Lammermoor*	Donizetti	Lucia
30	November	New York	*Lucia di Lammermoor*	Donizetti	Lucia
4	December	New York	*Lucia di Lammermoor*	Donizetti	Lucia
9	December	New York	*Lucia di Lammermoor*	Donizetti	Lucia
13	December	New York	*Lucia di Lammermoor*	Donizetti	Lucia

—— 1983 ——

DATE		PLACE	PERFORMANCE	COMPOSER	ROLE
10	January	Sydney	*Die Fledermaus*	J Strauss	Rosalinde
15	January	Sydney	Park Concert *Die Fledermaus*	J Strauss	Rosalinde
18	January	Sydney	*Die Fledermaus*	J Strauss	Rosalinde
23	January	Sydney	Concert		
5	February	Sydney	*Alcina*	Handel	Alcina
9	February	Sydney	*Alcina*	Handel	Alcina
12	February	Sydney	*Alcina*	Handel	Alcina
16	February	Sydney	*Alcina*	Handel	Alcina
19	February	Sydney	*Alcina*	Handel	Alcina
22	February	Sydney	*Alcina*	Handel	Alcina
26	February	Sydney	*Alcina*	Handel	Alcina
27	February	Sydney	Concert		
17	March	Genoa	*La Traviata* (incomplete)	Verdi	Violetta
22	**May**	**San Diego**	**Adriana Lecouvreur**	**Cilea**	**Adriana**
26	May	San Diego	*Adriana Lecouvreur*	Cilea	Adriana
29	May	San Diego	*Adriana Lecouvreur*	Cilea	Adriana
1	June	San Diego	*Adriana Lecouvreur*	Cilea	Adriana
12	June	Sydney	Concert		
25	June	Sydney	*Il Trovatore*	Verdi	Leonora
28	June	Sydney	*Il Trovatore*	Verdi	Leonora
2	July	Sydney	*Il Trovatore*	Verdi	Leonora
5	July	Sydney	*Il Trovatore*	Verdi	Leonora
8	July	Sydney	*Il Trovatore*	Verdi	Leonora
13	July	Sydney	*Il Trovatore*	Verdi	Leonora
16	July	Sydney	*Il Trovatore*	Verdi	Leonora
19	July	Sydney	*Il Trovatore*	Verdi	Leonora
22	July	Sydney	*Il Trovatore*	Verdi	Leonora
5	August	Sydney	*Semiramide*	Rossini	Semiramide
8	August	Sydney	*Semiramide*	Rossini	Semiramide
13	August	Sydney	*Semiramide*	Rossini	Semiramide
17	August	Sydney	*Semiramide*	Rossini	Semiramide
20	August	Sydney	*Semiramide*	Rossini	Semiramide
27	September	New York	*La Fille du Régiment*	Donizetti	Marie
1	October	New York	*La Fille du Régiment*	Donizetti	Marie
5	October	New York	*La Fille du Régiment*	Donizetti	Marie
8	October	New York	*La Fille du Régiment*	Donizetti	Marie
11	October	New York	*La Fille du Régiment*	Donizetti	Marie
14	October	New York	*La Fille du Régiment*	Donizetti	Marie
19	October	New York	*La Fille du Régiment*	Donizetti	Marie
22	October	New York	Metropolitan Opera Centenary Gala		
24	October	New York	*La Fille du Régiment*	Donizetti	Marie
28	November	London	*Esclarmonde*	Massenet	Esclarmonde
6	December	London	*Esclarmonde*	Massenet	Esclarmonde
10	December	London	*Esclarmonde*	Massenet	Esclarmonde
13	December	London	*Esclarmonde*	Massenet	Esclarmonde
16	December	London	*Esclarmonde*	Massenet	Esclarmonde

—— 1984 ——

DATE		PLACE	PERFORMANCE	COMPOSER	ROLE
14	January	Sydney	Park Concert *Lucia di Lammermoor*	Donizetti	Lucia
27	January	Sydney	*Adriana Lecouvreur*	Cilea	Adriana
30	January	Sydney	*Adriana Lecouvreur*	Cilea	Adriana
2	February	Sydney	*Adriana Lecouvreur*	Cilea	Adriana
7	February	Sydney	*Adriana Lecouvreur*	Cilea	Adriana
11	February	Sydney	*Adriana Lecouvreur*	Cilea	Adriana
14	February	Sydney	*Adriana Lecouvreur*	Cilea	Adriana
18	February	Sydney	*Adriana Lecouvreur*	Cilea	Adriana
22	February	Sydney	*Adriana Lecouvreur*	Cilea	Adriana
25	February	Sydney	*Adriana Lecouvreur*	Cilea	Adriana
29	February	Sydney	*Adriana Lecouvreur*	Cilea	Adriana
22	**May**	**Toronto**	**Anna Bolena**	**Donizetti**	**Anna**
25	May	Toronto	*Anna Bolena*	Donizetti	Anna
28	May	Toronto	*Anna Bolena*	Donizetti	Anna
31	May	Toronto	*Anna Bolena*	Donizetti	Anna
3	June	Toronto	*Anna Bolena*	Donizetti	Anna

DATE		PLACE	PERFORMANCE	COMPOSER	ROLE
6	June	Detroit	*Anna Bolena*	Donizetti	Anna
9	June	Detroit	*Anna Bolena*	Donizetti	Anna
21	June	San Diego	*I Masnadieri*	Verdi	Amelia
24	June	San Diego	*I Masnadieri*	Verdi	Amelia
30	June	San Diego	*I Masnadieri*	Verdi	Amelia
20	July	Sydney	*Les Contes d'Hoffmann*	Offenbach	Olympia, Giulietta, Antonia, Stella
23	July	Sydney	*Les Contes d'Hoffmann*	Offenbach	Olympia, Giulietta, Antonia, Stella
26	July	Sydney	*Les Contes d'Hoffmann*	Offenbach	Olympia, Giulietta, Antonia, Stella
30	July	Sydney	*Les Contes d'Hoffmann*	Offenbach	Olympia, Giulietta, Antonia, Stella
4	August	Sydney	*Les Contes d'Hoffmann*	Offenbach	Olympia, Giulietta, Antonia, Stella
7	August	Sydney	*Les Contes d'Hoffmann*	Offenbach	Olympia, Giulietta, Antonia, Stella
11	August	Sydney	*Les Contes d'Hoffmann*	Offenbach	Olympia, Giulietta, Antonia, Stella
15	August	Sydney	*Les Contes d'Hoffmann*	Offenbach	Olympia, Giulietta, Antonia, Stella
19	August	Sydney	Concert		
1	September	Sydney	*The Dialogues of the Carmelites*	Poulenc	Mme Lidoine
4	September	Sydney	*The Dialogues of the Carmelites*	Poulenc	Mme Lidoine
8	September	Sydney	*The Dialogues of the Carmelites*	Poulenc	Mme Lidoine
11	September	Sydney	*The Dialogues of the Carmelites*	Poulenc	Mme Lidoine
15	September	Sydney	*The Dialogues of the Carmelites*	Poulenc	Mme Lidoine
19	September	Sydney	*The Dialogues of the Carmelites*	Poulenc	Mme Lidoine
22	September	Sydney	*The Dialogues of the Carmelites*	Poulenc	Mme Lidoine
24	September	Sydney	*The Dialogues of the Carmelites*	Poulenc	Mme Lidoine
26	September	Sydney	*The Dialogues of the Carmelites*	Poulenc	Mme Lidoine
25	October	San Francisco	*Anna Bolena*	Donizetti	Anna
28	October	San Francisco	*Anna Bolena*	Donizetti	Anna
3	November	San Francisco	*Anna Bolena*	Donizetti	Anna
6	November	San Francisco	*Anna Bolena*	Donizetti	Anna
9	November	San Francisco	*Anna Bolena*	Donizetti	Anna
13	November	San Francisco	*Anna Bolena*	Donizetti	Anna

1985

DATE		PLACE	PERFORMANCE	COMPOSER	ROLE
12	January	Sydney	Park Concert *Les Contes d'Hoffmann*	Offenbach	Olympia, Giulietta, Antonia, Stella
22	January	Sydney	*Norma*	Bellini	Norma
26	January	Sydney	*Norma*	Bellini	Norma
29	January	Sydney	*Norma*	Bellini	Norma
2	February	Sydney	*Norma*	Bellini	Norma
9	February	Sydney	*Norma*	Bellini	Norma
12	February	Sydney	*Norma*	Bellini	Norma
16	February	Sydney	*Norma*	Bellini	Norma
27	March	Phoenix	Concert		
30	March	Atlantic City	Concert		
13	April	London	*Lucia di Lammermoor*	Donizetti	Lucia
16	April	London	*Lucia di Lammermoor*	Donizetti	Lucia
19	April	London	*Lucia di Lammermoor*	Donizetti	Lucia
23	April	London	*Lucia di Lammermoor*	Donizetti	Lucia
26	April	London	*Lucia di Lammermoor*	Donizetti	Lucia
24	May	Stockholm	Concert *Norma*	Bellini	Norma
9	June	Melbourne	Concert		
12	June	Sydney	Concert		
24	June	Sydney	*I Puritani*	Bellini	Elvira
28	June	Sydney	*I Puritani*	Bellini	Elvira
1	July	Sydney	*I Puritani*	Bellini	Elvira
6	July	Sydney	*I Puritani*	Bellini	Elvira
10	July	Sydney	*I Puritani*	Bellini	Elvira
13	July	Sydney	*I Puritani*	Bellini	Elvira
16	July	Sydney	*I Puritani*	Bellini	Elvira
4	**October**	**Toronto**	***Hamlet***	**Thomas**	**Ophélie**
7	October	Toronto	*Hamlet*	Thomas	Ophélie
10	October	Toronto	*Hamlet*	Thomas	Ophélie
13	October	Toronto	*Hamlet*	Thomas	Ophélie
16	October	Toronto	*Hamlet*	Thomas	Ophélie
19	October	Toronto	*Hamlet*	Thomas	Ophélie
30	October	Chicago	*Anna Bolena*	Donizetti	Anna
2	November	Chicago	*Anna Bolena*	Donizetti	Anna
5	November	Chicago	*Anna Bolena*	Donizetti	Anna
8	November	Chicago	*Anna Bolena*	Donizetti	Anna
11	November	Chicago	*Anna Bolena*	Donizetti	Anna
14	November	Chicago	*Anna Bolena*	Donizetti	Anna
19	November	Chicago	*Anna Bolena*	Donizetti	Anna
25	November	New York	Concert *Anna Bolena*	Donizetti	Anna
1	December	Boston	Concert *Anna Bolena*	Donizetti	Anna
6	December	Washington, DC	Concert *Anna Bolena*	Donizetti	Anna

DATE		PLACE	PERFORMANCE	COMPOSER	ROLE
— 1986 —					
10	January	Perth	Concert		
20	January	Sydney	Park Concert Rigoletto	Verdi	Gilda
28	January	Sydney	Lucia di Lammermoor	Donizetti	Lucia
1	February	Sydney	Lucia di Lammermoor	Donizetti	Lucia
8	February	Sydney	Lucia di Lammermoor	Donizetti	Lucia
14	February	Sydney	Lucia di Lammermoor	Donizetti	Lucia
19	February	Sydney	Lucia di Lammermoor	Donizetti	Lucia
5	March	Wellington	Concert		
8	March	Wellington	Concert		
21	April	Barcelona	Norma	Bellini	Norma
24	April	Barcelona	Norma	Bellini	Norma
27	April	Barcelona	Norma	Bellini	Norma
30	April	Barcelona	Norma	Bellini	Norma
5	June	Pittsburgh	La Fille du Régiment	Donizetti	Marie
7	June	Pittsburgh	La Fille du Régiment	Donizetti	Marie
10	June	Pittsburgh	La Fille du Régiment	Donizetti	Marie
19	June	Houston	Anna Bolena	Donizetti	Anna
22	June	Houston	Anna Bolena	Donizetti	Anna
25	June	Houston	Anna Bolena	Donizetti	Anna
28	June	Houston	Anna Bolena	Donizetti	Anna
22	July	Sydney	La Fille du Régiment	Donizetti	Marie
26	July	Sydney	La Fille du Régiment	Donizetti	Marie
30	July	Sydney	La Fille du Régiment	Donizetti	Marie
2	August	Sydney	La Fille du Régiment	Donizetti	Marie
9	August	Sydney	La Fille du Régiment	Donizetti	Marie
16	August	Sydney	La Fille du Régiment	Donizetti	Marie
23	August	Sydney	La Fille du Régiment	Donizetti	Marie
14	November	New York	I Puritani	Bellini	Elvira
18	November	New York	I Puritani	Bellini	Elvira
22	November	New York	I Puritani	Bellini	Elvira
25	November	New York	I Puritani	Bellini	Elvira
29	November	New York	I Puritani	Bellini	Elvira
3	December	New York	I Puritani	Bellini	Elvira
6	December	New York	I Puritani	Bellini	Elvira
9	December	New York	I Puritani	Bellini	Elvira
13	December	New York	I Puritani	Bellini	Elvira
18	December	New York	I Puritani	Bellini	Elvira
— 1987 —					
4	January	Wellington	Concert		
11	January	New York	Metropolitan Opera Gala		
15	January	Boston	Concert		
19	January	Pasadena	Concert		
23	January	San Diego	Concert		
27	January	Tulsa, Oklahoma	Concert		
1	February	Dallas	Concert		
5	February	Miami	Concert		
3	April	Toronto	Adriana Lecouvreur	Cilea	Adriana
6	April	Toronto	Adriana Lecouvreur	Cilea	Adriana
9	April	Toronto	Adriana Lecouvreur	Cilea	Adriana
12	April	Toronto	Adriana Lecouvreur	Cilea	Adriana
15	April	Toronto	Adriana Lecouvreur	Cilea	Adriana
18	April	Toronto	Adriana Lecouvreur	Cilea	Adriana
25	April	Houston	Concert		
8	June	Paris	Recital		
14	June	Warsaw	Recital		
25	September	Stockholm	Concert I Puritani	Bellini	Elvira
4	October	Glasgow	Concert		
7	October	Edinburgh	Concert		
25	October	New York	Concert		
12	November	New York	Il Trovatore	Verdi	Leonora
16	November	New York	Il Trovatore	Verdi	Leonora
20	November	New York	Il Trovatore	Verdi	Leonora
24	November	New York	Il Trovatore	Verdi	Leonora
27	November	New York	Il Trovatore	Verdi	Leonora
1	December	New York	Il Trovatore	Verdi	Leonora
5	December	New York	Il Trovatore	Verdi	Leonora
10	December	New York	Il Trovatore	Verdi	Leonora
16	December	New York	Il Trovatore	Verdi	Leonora
19	December	New York	Il Trovatore	Verdi	Leonora
— 1988 —					
21	January	Sydney	The Merry Widow	Lehar	Anna Glawari
28	January	Sydney	The Merry Widow	Lehar	Anna Glawari

DATE		PLACE	PERFORMANCE	COMPOSER	ROLE
3	February	Sydney	*The Merry Widow*	Lehar	Anna Glawari
12	February	Sydney	*The Merry Widow*	Lehar	Anna Glawari
17	February	Sydney	*The Merry Widow*	Lehar	Anna Glawari
19	February	Sydney	Recital		
23	February	Sydney	*The Merry Widow*	Lehar	Anna Glawari
6	March	Adelaide	Concert		
3	April	New York	Concert		
7	April	Syracuse	Concert		
15	April	Baltimore	Concert		
1	May	London	*Anna Bolena*	Donizetti	Anna
3	May	London	*Anna Bolena*	Donizetti	Anna
8	May	London	*Anna Bolena*	Donizetti	Anna
13	May	London	*Anna Bolena*	Donizetti	Anna
18	May	London	*Anna Bolena*	Donizetti	Anna
22	May	London	*Anna Bolena*	Donizetti	Anna
19	June	London	Royal Opera House John Tooley Gala		
5	July	Munich	Recital		
8	July	Catania	Recital		
21	October	Washington, DC	Concert		
24	October	New York	Concert		
30	October	New York	Concert		
21	November	Barcelona	*Lucia di Lammermoor*	Donizetti	Lucia
24	November	Barcelona	*Lucia di Lammermoor*	Donizetti	Lucia
27	November	Barcelona	*Lucia di Lammermoor*	Donizetti	Lucia
30	November	Barcelona	*Lucia di Lammermoor*	Donizetti	Lucia

—— 1989 ——

DATE		PLACE	PERFORMANCE	COMPOSER	ROLE
11	February	Costa Mesa, California	*Norma*	Bellini	Norma
15	February	Costa Mesa, California	Norma	Bellini	Norma
18	February	Costa Mesa, California	*Norma*	Bellini	Norma
24	February	Costa Mesa, California	*Norma*	Bellini	Norma
4	March	Jackson, Mississippi	Concert		
12	March	New York	Recital		
15	April	Detroit	*Norma*	Bellini	Norma
19	April	Detroit	*Norma*	Bellini	Norma
22	April	Detroit	*Norma*	Bellini	Norma
31	May	Barcelona	*Lucrezia Borgia*	Donizetti	Lucrezia
3	June	Barcelona	*Lucrezia Borgia*	Donizetti	Lucrezia
11	June	Barcelona	*Lucrezia Borgia*	Donizetti	Lucrezia
14	June	Barcelona	*Lucrezia Borgia*	Donizetti	Lucrezia
18	June	Paris	Concert *Lucrezia Borgia*	Donizetti	Lucrezia
15	July	Melbourne	Concert		
6	October	London	Recital		
11	October	Newcastle	Concert		
2	November	Dallas	*The Merry Widow*	Lehar	Anna Glawari
5	November	Dallas	*The Merry Widow*	Lehar	Anna Glawari
8	November	Dallas	*The Merry Widow*	Lehar	Anna Glawari
11	November	Dallas	*The Merry Widow*	Lehar	Anna Glawari
19	November	Hong Kong	Concert		

BIBLIOGRAPHY

Adams, Brian **La Stupenda,** Hutchinson Group, Victoria, 1980

Bonynge, Richard **Joan Sutherland, Designs for a Prima Donna,** The Craftsmens Press, Sydney, 1985

Braddon, Russell **Joan Sutherland,** Collins, Sydney, 1962

Caste Charles **Noël,** W.H. Allen, London, 1972

Christiansen, Rupert **Prima Donna, A History,** The Bodley Head, London, 1984

Eaton, Quaintance **Sutherland and Bonynge, An Intimate Biography,** Dodd Mead and Company, New York, 1987

Greenfield, Edward **Joan Sutherland,** Ian Allan, Sheperton Surrey, 1972

Hines, Jerome **Great Singers on Great Singing,** Doubleday & Company, New York, 1982

Kolodin, Irving **The Opera Omnibus,** E.P. Dutton, New York, 1976

Mackenzie, Barbara and Findlay **Singers of Australia,** Landsdowne Press, Melbourne, 1967

Major, Norma **Joan Sutherland,** Queen Anne Press, London, 1987

Rosenthal, Harold **Opera at Covent Garden,** Gollancz, London, 1967

Sutherland, Joan with Richard Bonynge **The Joan Sutherland Album,** The Craftsman House, Sydney, 1986

Tait, Viola **A Family of Brothers,** Heinemann, Melbourne, 1971

Warren-Smith, Neil with Frank Salter **25 Years of Australian Opera,** Oxford University Press, Melbourne, 1983

ACKNOWLEDGEMENTS

MANY PEOPLE have contributed to the production of this book on Dame Joan Sutherland's long and distinguished career. My thanks to Donald McDonald, General Manager of The Australian Opera; its Technical Administrator, Noel Staunton; my assistant David Crooks; Wendy Hill, Alex Burns, William Paterson and Shirley Germain.

The Art Gallery of New South Wales initiated the exhibition from which this book developed. My sincere thanks go to Edmund Capon, Gallery Director, for his enthusiasm and support, as well as to Diana Heath, Jan Meek, Avenel Mitchell and Brian Turner from the Gallery.

Any book is the result of many hours of often laborious, detailed work. The Honeysett Printing Group achieved tight deadlines without sacrificing quality, and I would especially like to thank Michele Bugden, Alan Hancock, Wayne Sheen, Annette Smith, Helen Stevenson and Louise Sufferini for their valuable contribution to the production. For proofreading, thanks to Tony Davies, Helen Barnes, Jeffrey Jones and Mark McDonnell. Furthermore, thanks to Harry Pears for attention to typography; and John Spatchurst and Meryl Blundell for assistance with design concepts.

For those who have contributed in other ways, I thank Qantas Airways Limited and the Sydney Inter-Continental Hotel; Christopher Brown and Jenny Kelly, Manufacturers' Mutual Insurance Limited, for financial assistance; Robyn Potter for her support; Ronald Horan, Ian Watchorn, Joseph Assaf and Staff of Ethnic Communications for invaluable translation services; Graham Cocks of Price Tiles for background images; and Lyndon Sayer-Jones for his legal expertise.

The book would not be what it is without the excellent photography commissioned by Honeysett Publications and I would like to extend my thanks to Greg Weight who photographed Dame Joan's costumes in the workshops, wardrobe stores and rehearsal studios of The Australian Opera Centre. Thanks also to Dallas Rowland and staff of Trannys; and Vic Foote and staff of Prestige Plates for converting Greg's photographs into the colour images that appear throughout the book.

I would like to thank all those who provided material for use in this book: the Archives Office of the Royal Opera House Covent Garden particularly the Archivist Francesca Franchi; The Australian Opera; the Theatre Museum of London; The Performing Arts Museum of the Victorian Arts Centre; the Canadian Opera Company; and Decca International. I remain indebted to all the photographers and designers who graciously agreed to allow reproduction of their images in this book.

The book would not have been possible without the teamwork and enthusiasm of Alan Davies, George Jaksic, Warren Wickman and Andrew Wilson. Finally, my thanks to Richard Bonynge and Joan Sutherland for their support and co-operation in providing material from their personal collection.

Moffatt Oxenbould

◉ Joan Sutherland after a concert in Wellington, New Zealand in March 1986. Photograph by Jocelyn Corlin.